Living with Loss

Living with Loss

A Minister's Memoir

Ernest L. Veal

PROVIDENCE HOUSE PUBLISHERS
Franklin, Tennessee

Copyright 1998 by Ernest Veal

All rights reserved. Written permission must be secured from the publisher to use or reproduce any part of this book, except for brief quotations in critical reviews or articles.

Printed in the United States of America

02   01   00   99   98   1   2   3   4   5

Library of Congress Catalog Card Number: 98-67680

ISBN: 1-57736-116-4

Cover design by Gary Bozeman

PROVIDENCE HOUSE PUBLISHERS
238 Seaboard Lane • Franklin, Tennessee 37067
800-321-5692

This publication is dedicated

to the Glory of God,

who after longevity of life, has endowed me
with the spiritual and physical resources
to pen this work
while considering the woeful tragedy
in my family.

To my beloved wife, Lucile,
following a cycle of sixty-two years
in marriage splendor,
yet possessing
the physical substance
in editing and copying my long hand,
word for word,
in her long hand,
in preparation for the typist.

To Brantley Joyce Christie
and Ruth Wilson Christie
for the excellence of their faith and character
in the unusual loss of their only brother,
mother and father
during the peak in life
while members of a model family of five.

Contents

Foreword—Marion M. Edwards ... ix
Foreword—Richard C. Looney ... xi
Acknowledgments ... xiii
Introduction ... xv

1. James Thomas Christie III ... 3
2. Joyce Veal Christie ... 21
3. James Thomas Christie Jr. ... 65
4. Inheritance Through Illness and Death ... 81

FOREWORD

Marion M. Edwards

JOYCE AND TOM CHRISTIE AND THEIR CHILDREN, BRANTLEY, Tom III, and Ruth were a much loved and admired family. They were an integral part of the Columbus, Georgia, community and especially of St. Luke United Methodist Church. Soon after my arrival as senior pastor at St. Luke in September 1988, I took note of the faithful presence of the Christie family in worship, always seated on a pew just below the pulpit.

Sadly, my personal relationship with this family began in response to the tragic and violent death of the young Christie son, Tom. He had just graduated from the University of Georgia and had begun his post-college job search. The aftershock of Tom's passing gave me pastoral opportunity to know, love, and struggle with the life-altering loss of their son and brother.

Unfortunately, before my pastorate at St. Luke was concluded eight years later in September 1996, death was to invade the immediate Christie family twice more, taking both mother, Joyce, and father, Tom, leaving Brantley and Ruth without their parents and brother. To this very day, family, friends, and pastors struggle with the Christie family tragedy asking the age-old question: "Why do bad things happen to good people?" However, I saw Tom and Joyce and their family handle this victoriously.

LIVING WITH LOSS

How fitting it is now, from the perspective of some time, for this family's tragic and heroic struggle to be shared by a family member who witnessed this episode unfold from an intimate perspective. The Reverend Ernest Veal, retired United Methodist minister, tells this story as only a father and grandfather could. It is a story of heroic faith worthy of being told. I am grateful to both Ernest and his wife, Lucile, for being faithfully present in the midst of this family tragedy. Thank you Ernest Veal, for your attempt to tell this story.

Bishop Marion M. Edwards
United Methodist Church
Raleigh, North Carolina

FOREWORD

Richard C. Looney

HERE IS TOLD THE INCREDIBLE STORY OF A FAMILY'S THREE-fold tragedy, and here also shines through a radiant faith that grows even in unbelievable sorrow and loss.

Ernest Veal tells the story of his family's triple tragedy. First, a beloved grandson, full of promise. Five years later, the beautiful daughter, the grandson's mother, dies of cancer. Two years later, the son-in-law dies with Lou Gehrig's disease.

This moving account gives a vivid picture of three very special people who die tragically. But overriding the tragedy is an uplifting account of faith expressed in the love and support of friends and the presence and power of God.

You will find yourself uplifted by the quiet and solid faith of a sorrowing family. You will also be moved to honor the God who sustains in sorrow and overcomes in death.

Bishop Richard C. Looney
United Methodist Church
Macon, Georgia

Acknowledgments

Persons about whom I must acknowledge assets for script preparation are as follows:

First, I am grateful for my wife's patient listening about material contents plus her copying and helpfulness about clarity of my thoughts.

In addition, I wish to acknowledge five different English teachers for proofreading as follows: Louise Jackson, Dawn Bray, Stephanie Jackson, and Loette Glisson in Wrightsville, Georgia, and Tina Epperson in Columbus, Georgia. Also to Mable Hester, secretary of St. Luke Church, during the events of woe in the Christie family. Furthermore, for Marci Tharpe's pleasant personality for typing and stenographical work. Much appreciation for contributing forewords for the publication: Bishop Marion Edwards, pastor of the Christie's at the time of the family's monumental struggles and Bishop Richard Looney, Resident Bishop for Brantley and Ruth Christie and the Veals in Macon, Georgia.

Lastly—and yet foremost—my eternal gratitude to Jesus Christ through God Almighty for the mental capacity and physical strength to complete the manuscript, over a two-year period.

INTRODUCTION

I WISH TO MAKE CLEAR THE ENERGY AND EFFORT EXPENDED IN preparing this publication must, on my part, meet two conditions. First any dividends derived through this work as profit, I will not accept personally. Whatever gain, if any, will be contributed to worthy causes. Second, although I am fortunate in health at the age of eighty-one, and I am a published author, I am aware no person is as alert mentally or physically in latter years as opposed to early life.

The chronicle I now unfold as a book was decided as I once shared the information with another individual. Said she, "That is very brave." She was correct, and I hesitate to come forth with a record which has deep melancholy potential. Nevertheless, while hesitating for a beginning, and following a period of laying back, I move forward. You will observe this book is written largely concerning the loss of loved ones while, at the same time, much emphasis is directed toward the loss of a child.

Another reason I must begin is founded in the serious challenging of friend or friends: "You must do it, there is no other person to do it." Thus I concluded if I do not, I will be very derelict in responsibility and duty. The writing itself is an honor and privilege, yet the time and energy involved with the manuscript required one to two years work in the face of keeping up with other privileges and involvement.

None of us are another St. Luke of the Bible. However, if any of us are to be active affirmatists of the Holy Spirit, then constantly we are compelled to follow instructions of spiritual declaration. We all are St. Lukes to some degree.

Recorded in the outset of the great physician's writing is the statement in which he declares, since he was present in certain experiences and an eyewitness, he is compelled to share his foreknowledge in light of how his own view and testimony could be rewarding to others of that day, as well as future posterity (Luke 1:14 paraphrased).

If St. Luke had disobeyed the Holy Spirit, thus failing to inscribe and document on scroll what he had seen and heard, then the Christian movement would have been weakened. Each of us often must testify to what we have seen and heard, both spiritual and civic events.

Any Godly person trying to describe or explain the work of the Holy Spirit will agree that work of such manifestation is not easily characterized. Jesus Christ himself suggested one could compare such spiritual presence to the wind which is totally indescribable. One element in which all of us would agree is the Holy Spirit is a powerful force. Thus I must begin!

As a published author, my hesitancy to convey this record is unconventional inasmuch as I am treating circumstances involving my own immediate family. Trying to be modest about something which may seem immodest is difficult.

The human mind is quick to grab variations of literary composites. We make reading decisions in light of what appeals to our preferable desires. Novels, for example, are mostly attractive light reading, including suspense, which of course requires gifted authors. Zane Grey long ago penned a book about early civilization. As a teenager with limited knowledge, I concluded I was reading real true information. Zane Grey was a gifted writer as are others in the field of fiction.

Introduction

Another concern in this material that I must respect is the mother who is the central role of what happened. This mother insisted nothing ever be said or done regarding her life in any form except something which glorified God and her wonderful savior, Jesus Christ. One month prior to my daughter's heavenly ascension, we were alone. I stated, "Joyce, something should be written about your life." In her humble attitude she answered, "I haven't done anything." Her father felt differently. Secondly, I asked permission for her parents to make a sizeable contribution in memorial to her family. The contribution was simple and easy to process—the writing was different. For months I struggled with indecision as to whether I should begin or not. I shall in this work be very sensitive to that person's wishes and her profound humility.

Therefore, I believe this narrative will show forth, in each line, statements and thoughts which not only represent heavy reading, yet at the same time include passages which stimulate and inspire spiritual and physical elevation. In some sense, it becomes heavenly and promotes a sense of acceptance and place in our misfortunes.

In our daily proceedings, often another person's decisions, example, and foresight send wave lengths into our hearts which, in turn, awaken and cause us to respond toward quality determination. Such moves in our life implant in our minds a sense of peace and serenity of acceptance in our times of trouble. They also set in motion our resolve to continue our earthly pilgrimage at our best, no matter what befalls us.

This writing was born not only in the loss of a child but in the devastation of losing a family. The following disclosure is an account regarding the unusual story of the Christie family in Columbus, Georgia. This is information I feel compelled to share. Thus I commit myself to the duty as well as the privilege.

I hope I will not turn you away, but this publication is not casual or easy going. The conveying of the following

LIVING WITH LOSS

happenings are somewhat like the psalmist David offered us when he wrote "God is our refuge and strength, a very present help in trouble. Therefore will not we fear though the earth be removed and though the mountains be carried into the midst of the sea. Though the waters therefore roar and be troubled, though the mountains shake with the swelling thereof" (Psalm 46: 1–3).

This fact makes this book a little more difficult in self-restraint. I must adjust my pattern and style, as author and columnist inasmuch as my pattern and self-nature includes both solemnity and insincerity, both casual and formal. Some people, in reading some things I have written, have stated, "It made me laugh awhile and cry awhile." In this book there isn't much room for laughter. The work is a version of a model family in which circumstances came to pass in a matter of a few years developing into what so many immediate friends termed "total disbelief." These conditions are those which ministers, physicians, civic leaders, and other principal interpreters termed as "indescribable." One disaster followed another. One magnitude after another of painful confrontation for a single family. Yet, we managed through leaning on the magnitude of God's sufficient grace.

I wish to preface my remarks about the Christie household by laying out some personal burden. As a clergyman, I ministered to parents who had lost a child, something I personally never encountered for a continued period of fifty-four years. My wife and I were fortunate.

All of us hold in our acquaintance parents who have labored from the outset in losing a child. For instance, at the time of birth. The joy of God's precious gift vanishes immediately. Parents behold the life of their own flesh and blood having passed through what we know as death so quickly.

Why is it? So many mothers and fathers imply sometimes that the death of a child is more frustrating to manage than the death of a husband or wife or just another loved one.

Introduction

The profoundness which comes down upon us in the loss of a son or daughter can be credited to the eternal truth that there is no other condition whereby we are dealing so intimately with our own flesh and blood. Childbirth links us up with Godly creation more distinctly than any other human relationship.

The comment of the late Bishop Arthur J. Moore once drew my attention: "If you have any conflict regarding the immortality of the soul, just wait until a child comes into your life, penetrates the tenderness of your heart, weaves its fingertips through your hair, and then all of a sudden vanishes from your presence. Your everything takes flight out of your reach, extends into eternity." Then, said the great preacher, "Your second thoughts about the immortality of the soul will not linger." To me, what the minister meant was no doubt regarding destiny of the soul—your doubts will be replaced by sound affirmation about the eternity of the soul and its heavenly state.

Have you ever lost a child? The answer to this question can be quickly fashioned by multitudes ever since the outset of civilization—there are so many traps through which a life can be quickly stilled.

Grant, if you will, my attempt to be inclusive of many out there who are trying to adjust to some excruciating tribulation. Surely, through the love of God, you are including in his mercy that "I have come thus far by the grace of God, I can go on." Hopefully, in that spiritual environment, at times you are surprised how well you are managing in such a dilemma. A relief will come through peace, not of this world, but through the Prince of Peace.

To be sure, the degree of suffering in the death of our offspring is often affected through how it came to pass. Circumstances in death alter the lead of mental impoundment. Every day parents and loved ones are present around other loved ones who suffer some terminal disease. Twenty-four hours pass slowly, followed by the oncoming day. The

Living with Loss

beloved individual experiences no improvement. Time goes on; each day seemingly becomes sinking sand. Medical science exhausts potential helpful procedure.

However, the candle of hope doesn't burn out—even when the future remains so bleak. Relatives, friends, and neighbors drop in. Then begins the quietness, the loneliness of fading evening, including broken sleep during the night. Chores which loved ones in attendance welcome as a privilege offer at least some opportunity to alter the outcome.

Consider the case of Rod Carew, who like many in similar circumstances struggled with the needs of a child born with a serious organic problem. Mr. Carew, a renowned baseball player, painfully lost his daughter while medical science ran out of time searching for a bone marrow transplant.

There are other factors in the loss of a child or family member in an untimely death that cause one to enter mental shock. There is the auto crash, the violence of evil set forth in the use of firearms and explosives of some wicked device, the aircraft which did not make it, and many other unfortunate happenings causing our mental faculties enormous strain and agitation.

In the sudden death of a daughter or a son or others, we think that if we had only been there perhaps there was something we could have offered, some helpful execution of love which would have been cherished.

No one can evaluate whether death caused by a continued degree of illness or a sudden, completely unexpected illness or accident is the most difficult to accept. Which is the greatest uphill burden? We understand so little about death. There are some aspects of existence we seemingly are not worthy to know. The Scripture promises comprehension ultimately but not immediately. We know Jesus said, "Let not your heart be troubled, ye believe in God believe also in me" (John 14:1).

In either case, at some length of suffering the mind can stir a degree of tranquility, and we are surprised "as the peace of

Introduction

God which passes all understanding" makes possible the pulling together of one's self, recreating somewhat a degree of balance and function.

As previously stated, I lived a long time before facing the loss of a child. However, in my role in life, I shared the burden of others who had been less fortunate. Allow me to share two or three illustrations of other people's problems.

It was a beautiful spring afternoon. The farming season was in full swing. Five-year-old Marvette Bailey and her parents were aboard a mule-drawn wagon on their way to some farm chores. Peace and tranquility of mind aptly described the family's togetherness. Tragedy was the farthest thought from their minds, and then it happened! Marvette fell overboard.

The father dashed to secure an automobile, and soon they had driven six miles to a doctor's office. Although a wagon wheel had passed across Marvette's body, examinations indicated she would be O.K. Upon second consideration, there was a feeling that getting to a hospital would be wise. Medical services in the 1940s were far less available and affordable than today; insurance was a problem. However, the parents made it to the hospital in good state. But in the afternoon they were crushed. Internal injuries caused Marvette's death.

As mentioned previously, my early background with Marvette's parents, long before my marriage and my entering the ministry, prompted the father and mother to call me to their home. I was privileged to share the loss of their loving child and officiate in the funeral. Upon reaching the residence, in a bedroom sat my friend Marcus. Emotionally distraught, the father's words remain in my mind, "I killed my own child." Of course his conclusion was not true, but that was the way he felt. False guilt quickly enters the mind after such a tragedy.

Today, those two parents would be quick to tell you nothing ever happened to them which came close to causing

Living with Loss

the lifetime hurt as did the loss of their child, although other disasters occurred. Other parents can confirm the same.

Yet, in the suffering of the Bailey family, some good things happened. Life went on, and years later I participated in the funeral celebration for Marcus after sixty-three years of marriage.

Another tragedy so frequently experienced by parents is the death of a teenage child. There are readers of this material who have answered the phone and suddenly, for a moment, their world turned upside down. They were shaken and dumfounded while bearing a message from some informant at the other end of the line. If you faced such trauma, perhaps you learned of your precious youth's disaster through some other media. No matter what, such conveyance is earth-shaking. The tremendous numbness is hard to handle; parents find themselves reaching out to each other with circumstances they never expected to face. They try to find something to steady their course while the tide of great tragedy is attacking their paradise.

Debbie's family experienced her loss through a teenage tragedy. She was, as I saw her, the queen of the community at home, school, church, wherever. If anyone was ever plucked from a wonderful, gratifying life while a pilgrim on this earth, it was this girl. Her life was based on enduring values and eternal qualities, rather than a passing fad. And then it happened, an automobile crash led to incredible suffering and eventually the end of another young and tender life.

During the frontier days of America, the tragedy of mortality at an early age was prevalent. It was not unusual for mothers to birth as many as fifteen children and only 60 or 70 percent reached adulthood. This, of course, was due to limited medical help and poor parental education.

It is mind boggling to remind oneself how so many parents have lost a child in war alone. My grandfather Veal was a soldier in the great Civil War. Included in his children

Introduction

were five sons. During the national conflict, three of the five were engaged in struggle. In one battle one of the sons received gunfire to the body. History records his last words were, "Oh father, I cannot go on." Yes, what an awful way to lose a child.

In our society, during the late 1990s, the death of the young caused by a totally different lifestyle is appalling. As a young man, I never heard or witnessed teenagers committing bodily harm to one another. True there were conflicts, but generally speaking, differences were settled without damage. Today we are exposed to nontraditional philosophies and lifestyles resulting in preventable calamities. In former periods, lack of medical and scientific knowledge and opportunities was the chief culprit of youthful casualties. The modern day explosion of hate, envy, and greed is expressed through firearms. Use of intoxicating alcohol and other drugs is instrumental in marching parents to the hospital and, perhaps, graveside with wounded hearts never to be the same again.

Recently, I was walking down Broughton Street in Savannah, Georgia. In recent years, modern transition has developed Broughton and the nearby Savannah riverfront into an attractive tourist activity.

The date was Tuesday, July 9, 1996. The Olympic torch would proceed from the Atlantic Ocean up the Savannah River Channel. The torch was to be born or carried by selected persons proceeding ashore into the state of Georgia. Needless to say, as I walked down Broughton Street, people were excited. Among others, the state governor and the Olympic committee chairman from Atlanta were present for the celebration. Young parents with their cute youngsters were all smiles, enjoying an event filled with history and anticipation. Suddenly my feathers fell.

A picture stored in my mind years before sprang forth. The mental flash reminded me of an earlier date when I was

Living with Loss

walking in that identical place and something terrible happened. At that point, the police, as well as others, were dashing to and fro with stretchers, moving bodies from the building.

A father and son were proprietors of a small business. Just before I arrived, one or more persons had entered the building and demanded the cash register contents. As I learned later, not only the father and son were present but also the wife and mother.

It was reported that the mother challenged the criminals who in turn shot to death her husband and son. This illustration is one of many where deep tragedy had made its ugly mark, leaving a mother who not only had lost a son but also a husband. Although I did not know the family and the outcome of mother and wife, the action compounded her mind and may have broken her health and possibly hastened her death.

On Sixteenth Street in Columbus, Georgia, a residential building stands along beside other similar structures. The subject I refer to represents other residential developments set forth in the 1920s. These diverse frame buildings vary in architectural design, some one floor, some two floors. They vary in exterior patterns and are positioned about equal distance apart from the city sidewalk.

Each unit is usually well manicured through the art of those who hold the deed for the property. They vary in esteem. Seldom is one vacant. The environment is very peaceful and serene. Beautiful ancient oak trees display individual personality. People walk to and fro on sidewalks and neat lawns.

May 11, 1996, the prelude to Mother's Day, I am pushing this pen as my body is supported in a small cane bottomed chair around an eating table located in a breakfast room. About the furniture I'm using, I know not the date. I do know such furnishings grab my mental faculties.

Introduction

You enjoy, very likely, your own pieces which never grow old. The house I'm in includes piece after piece unique in nature.

This is the Christie family residence. Here a father, a mother, a son, and two daughters lived when all the ingredients expected in a model family were displayed.

Back of every household there is a beginning. As you read these thoughts on how the Christie family began, I trust the information will be helpful. How two persons met, followed by matrimony, is always attractive. Likely you recall that time yourself.

Living with Loss

CHAPTER ONE

James Thomas Christie III

JOYCE VEAL, A FRESH GRADUATE, HAVING RECENTLY EARNED her degree in music from Wesleyan College of Arts in Macon, Georgia, in 1961 had moved with her family into the Methodist parsonage in Sandersville, Georgia. The graduate's next move was seeking employment for teaching public school music. That effort resulted in a job with Muscogee County Schools in Columbus, Georgia.

The mother of the young teacher traveled with her daughter the 157 miles for companionship and to help her secure an apartment. Late in the afternoon a fatigued mother and daughter had not established residence. Someone had informed her of a young man, Tom Christie Jr., who was a realtor. She had not planned to contact the realtor, nevertheless, the two made a call to the gentleman seeking assistance. In turn, while trying to be helpful, the young realtor sent someone to show Joyce an apartment, which she selected as her new residence.

Later, the young musician and realtor became acquainted. That developed romance, leading to matrimony at the altar of the United Methodist Church in Sandersville, Georgia.

Living with Loss

Some of you taking time to read this can quickly rehash moments leading up to the marriage of your own child: a significant event meaning much to you, and an occasion when you were both sad and joyful. The momentous occasion forces attention upon your son's or daughter's life. To be sure, it is another milestone, the beginning of a family unit. Newlyweds always draw attention.

Forgive me for failing to resist the temptation of alluding to the marital alliance of my own daughter. Over the long road through matrimony, I had shared the experience of some daughters, parents, and grandparents. As a minister I have been honored to witness many marriages.

The time had come on June 16, 1963, for me to pass the hand of my child into the hands of a young man in whom I had the utmost confidence. Often I had watched other parents do this. On June 16, my turn arrived. Many a father has felt and shared the same and fully understands what I mean.

The stained glass windows of the church, engraved symbols of the Christian faith, were at their very best. Between the altar rail and the chancel stood a clergyman there to assist the pastor. Already down the aisles of the sanctuary, movement had begun.

In the narrow vestibule of the church, the bride patiently waited on the arm of her father. My daughter's hand was a little nervous. I offered my touch of reassurance. I've been there often in a wedding, thus I could manage my privilege and responsibility, so I gathered. After yielding Joyce to her future husband, it was my move to appear inside the altar rail. Then I was to resume from the assisting clergyman my privilege to continue the ceremony. At that point I did an about-face, looking directly into the countenance of my own daughter. I had always beheld the radiance and charm of other fathers' daughters, but this time the procedure was reversed. Of all things, I stammered and struggled with the Lord's Prayer the first time in my life, but I recovered immediately.

James Thomas Christie III

You see there are two potentially serious times in life which most parents may or may not encounter. One may be more serious than the other. One may be joyful, the other heartbreaking. Nevertheless, both happen at a time of solemnity or Godly reverence. The two are namely matrimony and death. One is yielding to another person and the other, in death, yielding to God.

Never, on that memorable wedding day June 16, 1963, in the year of our Lord, did the couple whom I write about ever expect in their wildest of dreams that, down the long road, fate would come down upon them so hard.

As you know, the marriage ceremony includes, "What God has joined together, let no man put asunder." From the altar, the young husband and wife moved on to their residence on Sixteenth Street, Columbus, Georgia. It was there showers of blessings began to fall upon them, untold.

Down the line, the new family was well and blessed by the grace of God to a point I had never seen excelled. In the family I viewed physical and economical success, a blanket of tender care, concern, love, and affection unsurpassed. Never in my presence with that group, although I wasn't always there, did I ever hear an unkind word or a raised voice. I saw the best education which offered unexcelled opportunities. In this family was a chosen church home, St. Luke United Methodist. The family sat together in about the same place each Sunday, third pew from the front in a large sanctuary. This was togetherness at its best.

This was the beginning of what came to pass, for the family children were James Thomas Christie III, Joyce Brantley Christie, and Ruth Wilson Christie. Like other young couples, Joyce and Tom made sure their offsprings' names included the epithet of their parents and grandparents: Mr. and Mrs. Tom Christie Sr.; Reverend and Mrs. Ernest Veal.

From the outset of family life, the career of the wife, professionally speaking, was discontinued. The decision was

LIVING WITH LOSS

the preference of both father and mother. In 1963, the Sixteenth Street homes were occupied largely by older occupants, thus no young adults or children. As the years passed, the complexion altered and, as the older residents were making adjustments and experiencing termination of life, young adults purchased property and settled around the family about whom I write. Both Joyce and Tom had winsome personalities and thus accumulated a multitude of friends.

THOMAS III—THE CHILD

On November 13, 1965, the birth of James Thomas Christie III transcended life anew for Tom and Joyce Christie. They became parents for the first time. Furthermore, no individual is propelled into motion on this planet without four grandparents, among the quick or deceased.

The Grandmother Veal of Tom Christie III went happily to the Christie home, an opportunity all devoted grandmothers welcome. By the same token, young mothers prefer, of all people to be present in their miraculous experience of motherhood, the individual whose flesh and blood ushered them into the world—their own mothers—especially during the drama of their first born.

When the contribution my wife made to her daughter was finished, she planned to ride ninety miles by bus home. This was a day when aircraft services weren't yet deeply set in. Her son-in-law, whom we later lost in death, was so appreciative he insisted in placing his mother-in-law on an airplane, but nevertheless the road trip by bus proved adequate. The child, like your child, began to mature toward adolescence and adulthood.

As a grandfather, at this point I risk being immodest. Be that as it may, this publication carries such a heavy burden in illustration, perhaps I can elude with a little light-hearted verbiage.

James Thomas Christie III

As already implied, the norm for grandparents is to lift a photo from a pocket and show off a grand-youngster. One grandfather, as perhaps you have heard stated said, "If I had been knowledgeable about how splendid grandchildren are, I would have had them first."

One can certainly have a fulfilling life and never become a parent or grandparent, but it helps. Enjoying being a grandparent is usually excitement blown completely out of proportion.

You grandpas and grandmas out there have experienced such an illustration as follows: While our first granddaughter was a small child, during a family visit, she could not be left with us overnight because her father loved his children so ardently, there was no way he could go home without them. My wife told me recently how the parents managed as the child cried not to go home. Her mother and father pacified the child through promising, as they arrived back home, they would arrange for her to talk to us by telephone. I bet many of you reading this have had the same experience. Grandchildren respond to their grandparents.

While my work included a pastorate at Trinity Church in Warner Robins, I had returned to a former parish to officiate at a wedding. In my absence, little Tom, while visiting, inquired, "Where is Granddaddy?" My wife answered, "He has gone to marry someone." The child began to whimper and said, "But Granddaddy is already married."

In another pastorate (following a weekend) I observed the church register. The same lad had his name and to the right of the page had written "The preacher's grandson." If he was searching for attention, he claimed mine. Any granddaddy understands what I'm saying. If you have not done so already, do not fail to record early remarks of your children and grandchildren.

I had ventured to my wife, that if times of some great misfortune were to occur in this ideal household, how could

Living with Loss

they cope with it? Yet in a span of a few years not one but three misfortunes came tumbling down on our family.

THE FIRST OF THREE WEEKENDS
OCTOBER 8–10, 1988

All three of the almost unbearable events in the Christie family occurred during the season of fall.

The first began on Saturday morning, October 8, 1988. I had gone to a local cemetery where I had been so often as a lad, and later in an official capacity to deliver eulogies.

Liberty Grove Cemetery represented my heritage and background. At times, like so many places of burial, vegetation and growth had taken charge. I had learned that Saturday, October 8, had been scheduled as clean-up day. I showed up and upon returning to my residence at about 11:00 A.M., the telephone rang. Little did I know I would hear such shocking information. Many of you have received such news one never forgets; often earth-shaking.

The receiver revealed the voice of our oldest daughter, Joyce. The mother of Tom Christie III was calling from Athens, Georgia, the site of the University of Georgia. Said Joyce, at first with good voice balance, "Daddy, last night little Tom decided he didn't want to live, and he attempted to take his life." Then a broken voice began to skip and quiver as she continued, "The doctors do not think he will live." Earlier that morning someone had informed Tom and Joyce of the tragedy regarding their twenty-two year old son. The Christie's were flown immediately in a company aircraft the 150 miles to the hospital.

In some circumstances of death, we immediately assume: "If I could have been there, maybe there was something I could have said, some move I could have made which would have blocked or prevented what happened." In many instances it is true; one or more persons with

James Thomas Christie III

opportunity could have shifted the course, and tragedy could have been avoided. The problem is no one should dwell too much on what we call the big "IF." What we must do, as someone said, is to pray for courage to accept what we cannot change.

Lucile and I traveled hurriedly, of course, to Athens. We parked in the hospital vehicle area. Following a brief period of crying, we pulled ourselves together. I voiced how many times I have appeared at a medical facility as clergy, privileged to share the burden of others as they struggled to cope with adversities affecting mind and soul. To my wife I said, "Today it is us! The case is ours." From that we could better understand how others have made their way through like difficult conditions.

On the curb of the hospital entrance, our son-in-law sat with his face buried in his hands. As we approached, his eyes met ours. The first of three tragedies in the family had come to pass. Said a broken father the simple words, "He is gone." Millions of fathers like this father have heard, "He or she is gone." Parents have asked or been tempted to ask, why? Persons have shed oceans of tears.

Before us was the loss of another young life. In this case the first born and only son, sibling of two sisters. The big brother of a little one born late in life, senior to a little sister who reached out to a young man strong and tall. Another sister near his age loved with warm affection.

Words cannot satisfy or adjectives describe the diversity of hurt coming down upon parents who face not only the loss of a child, but especially when death is thought of as a preferable choice—no desire for earthly pilgrimage. In this case the misery of a father who emphasized family values, loving a son who was the only individual to carry on the Christie name. For this father, a world crumbled.

On that fateful Saturday, we were invited to travel on the plane back to the family residence. But, it was necessary for us to return to our home, and then to Columbus.

LIVING WITH LOSS

Sixteenth street quickly became crowded with friends and neighbors, as often happens when others are in trouble; people from all walks of life: teachers, dentists, ministers, psychiatrists, homemakers. The humble, radiant qualities of Joyce and Tom Christie had reached into the hearts of everyone—housekeepers, lawn maintenance persons—a very inclusive broad base of friends.

On Monday, a memorial service would be held, led by the Reverend Marion Edwards, D.D., now Bishop Edwards, along with Virginia Calhoun of the laity. Just as this tragic situation had occurred, it would be repeated two more times. No one in their wildest imagination could comprehend such would occur to the same family. Yet, there awaited two more happenings yet to unfold.

In these trying times, certainly we would crash if that innate desire to "Bear ye one another's burden," (Gal. 6:2) was absent. It should be and has always been: when one of us hurts, we should all hurt. When one of us rejoices or succeeds we should all feel victorious. Survival is often found through the kind words and embracing arms of others. It is God's exercise through which, often times, a load is lifted. It was Roy Rogers who stated years ago, "A shared burden is a lighter burden." Small unit support groups have kept our ship afloat. I submit to you we can always measure the worth of another through that person's sensitivity to suffering. The whole wide world is full of inhabitants with warm hearts.

Isn't it better that God, in his plan for our lives, did not open himself completely by telling us what would happen to us along the way?

The next day following the death of our beloved grandson, one thing I did know was I needed the church. I needed St. Luke; I yearned for their support and found it. This was the church home for this young family and still is.

Sunday, October 10, was the regularly scheduled day for Holy Communion. At the altar, the elements of celebration,

James Thomas Christie III

symbolizing the death and resurrection of Jesus, offered strength which all of us have often received. The celebration occurred at the close of the service, and standing after kneeling, I exited alone by the side door. But I wasn't alone; any Christian understands. Furthermore, in that worship service (while our son-in-law an illustration of good health) I did not know in less than two years, on September 3, 1995, I would again worship in the same congregation on Sunday morning and hear the same pastor announce the funeral schedule for our son-in-law the next day, Monday.

The next day, the presence of Tom III's young fraternity friends inspired me. In the first place, they came forth to their comrade's hometown for his memorial services. Then they made it a point to travel some distance to the site of internment.

Not for the remainder of my life will I forget that group of young men dressed in their best as they stood in a cluster near their friend's gravesite; young gentlemen with tender hearts, crushed. There they stood, one single body bunched together. This was an encounter where they did not waver; this was an important class meeting to them, one they dared not cut.

On Monday they were not finished. The next day, on their own initiative, they put together a memorial service at the First Methodist Church in Athens, Georgia. My wife and I did not attend, but a tape was produced. As you know, there is no recording so somber as one bringing out the sound and ritual of funeral. Although many large congregations have a policy of taping all eulogies held in the church edifices, the transcript in this case represented a very serious hour for these college students. The notations rendered such a definite solemn background. Faintly, the tape brought out the audible sobbing of college youth. On listening to the presentation, I could easily detect the feelings of a youthful audience, manifested in circumstances of disbelief.

LIVING WITH LOSS

The service, like others, was not only an expression of reverence and worship but, in addition, an outlet where they, like all of us, can let the soul weep, whereby some grief can escape. I do not recall all that was mentioned in their testimonies which were at times faintly recorded. However, the comments of the principal address near the microphone were very audible. The speaker used three objectives as he valued his friend Tom Christie III's life. They were: intelligent, handsome, and humble.

HE WAS INTELLIGENT

All of us take pride in the appraisal of our children. When they excel in the classroom or otherwise, or parents observe a report coming home for their consideration. I've never seen a mother or father down-spirited when a son or a daughter penetrates the dean's list, role of honor, or in some instances, puts across just the need of a passing grade. We like to share the academic victory of persons, whether it relates to our families or others. Teachers and coaches are excited when someone they have tutored grades out well.

Nonetheless, we all admit there is a vast differential in knowledge and wisdom. Knowledge without prudence is cramped, while if you integrate intelligence with wisdom, you have a rewarding, unlimited combination.

The following is an illustration that no matter what we accomplish academically, prudence is also a must for success and the good life.

We are all familiar with St. Paul's words in the Scriptures where he speaks of love as utmost: "Though I speak with the tongues of men and of angels and have not love, I am become sounding brass or a tinkling symbol. And though I have the gift of prophecy and understand all

James Thomas Christie III

mysteries and all knowledge: and though I have faith so that I could remove mountains and have not charity, I am nothing" (1 Corinthians 13:1–5).

In this passage, St. Paul assimilates a comparison of knowledge and charity, with charity being utmost.

Anyone of us can readily agree—intelligence and wisdom can be treated in the same fashion, with wisdom as frontrunner, while both prudence and intelligence are serious components.

Reliance upon St. Paul's truth is wise since he himself was our best interpreter of what is essential in life. The author of thirteen books of the Bible was schooled in Tarsus, the city of intellectual learning. The law was sufficient for his goal until he was unexpectedly interceded on his way to Damascus to protest the work of the Holy Spirit. Jesus, the Light, instantly, plainly showed him his lack of love, wisdom, and understanding. With his high station and education, his writings became an instrument through which he could best effectuate his possession of this new knowledge.

Often there comes a time in our lives when neither intelligence nor wisdom is in control. The moment when our thinking was not in focus, and we acted impulsively, either premeditated or not, may set off some rage or anger. We commit an act not retraceable. If we have a chance, we rationalize, "I was out of my mind."

Furthermore, we find this to be true in diseases diagnosed as mental problems. In such cases, we may make a move altogether abnormal. This was the case with my grandson, or yours, or other members of our families when neither intelligence nor wisdom are active. In this mental state we are helpless; decisions are made when we are not responsible. Yet irresponsible, we conclude our dreams are helpless. What is utmost, we gather, can never transpire or come to pass; then one becomes hopeless and helpless while alone and thus has no desire to live.

Living with Loss

Have you ever stopped for a moment and considered the extent of how anything which goes through our hands shapes our future? We are quite well schooled about something entering our mouths, what is good or harmful for us. "Don't put that in your mouth," we point out to a small child. The wisdom and intelligence of how we deal with something we hold in our hand is paramount.

Consider our physicians; through addition, not deduction, they determine a diagnosis about a patient's illness. Intelligence has produced information and knowledge, and surgery comes into play.

The next move involves wisdom. Whether a surgeon should place or not place in their hands a surgical tool. What is the wise thing to do? This process goes on in everyday thought.

When our grandson appeared upon a college campus the fall quarter of 1983, his grandmother Veal was like any other grandmother, eager about his future. She took time to pen him a letter. The principal subject of the correspondence was her concern regarding drugs in substances, primarily alcohol. His first letter to our house from college, November 1983, to his grandmother, verbatim, went as follows:

"Don't worry; there isn't much of a temptation for evil in my fraternity. It is true, alcohol is used by some members, but they certainly do not force it upon anyone. There are some people like me who choose not to drink." What the fine young man did about his commitment is not in my knowledge altogether. What I do know is, in almost all things which affect us, through our hands must pass.

Firearms are usually held in the hands proceeding use. Food reaches the body first being held in the hand. It's a continuous process. Christian symbolism is often displayed through the thought of God in His great power holding us in His hands. God holds us in the palm of his hands as we go step-by-step, day-by-day, whatever we face.

James Thomas Christie III

HE WAS HANDSOME

Not only do we respond favorably to our children being considered intelligent but, likewise, to have someone evaluate affirmatively their appearance. It causes us satisfaction when another person makes encouraging comments regarding our exposure. Also, other forms which bring out an asset of how someone views our personhood is motivating.

Appearance is more or less the bottom line of anything. The person who does not respond to kind phrases such as "you look distinguished," "you are pretty," "I've just been sitting here admiring your hair," may not be alive. Every individual enjoys hearing words of this nature. They are music to our ears.

Name some enterprise which emphasizes the birds-eye view in all perception, and you include all commerce. The automobile industry rolls out its new subject, aimed at grabbing the eye. Take a vacation or travel, and wherever you go, there will be a very large sign which reads, "Scenic Route."

The fashion show is designed to attract and promote wholesome exposure and spectacle. Festivals arrange exhibits for viewers' pleasure and entertainment. The jacket on the book is a cover to promote and distribute its attractiveness. Two people's perception about each other is a vital part in developing matrimony. The illustrations we've just considered are both physical and spiritual. Engaging in this kind of philosophy is enhancing toward happiness, gratification, and fulfillment.

Furthermore, if one will glance in the direction of the Scriptures, there is tremendous evidence of God's delight in appearance. Genesis 29:17 speaks about the beauty of Rachel. In Esther 2:7 her beauty is mentioned. Our bodies are created beautifully. This offers appreciation of our worth in sight. Proverbs 20:29 reads, "The beauty of old men is the gray head." Also the following is indeed impressive: "Let the beauty of our Lord be upon us" (Ps. 90:17). One other reference, in speaking of Jesus, Isaiah 52:7 says, "How beautiful upon the mountains are the feet of him that bringeth good tidings of good, that publishes salvation, and sayeth unto Zion, 'Thy God reigneth,' radiance."

While making reference about two beautiful women of the Old Testament, the Scripture also lifts up the pitfall of beauty if it is only what we call skin deep. "Favor is deceitful, beauty if vain" (Prov. 31:30). In addition, "Lust not after beauty in the heart" (Prov. 6:25).

In the Creator's work, God made everyone beautiful. I've never heard two parents who looked upon a child born unto them and said, "Isn't our child hideous." All of us are beautiful in God's sight. The miracle of his work indeed takes us aback. My child, yours, and others may not be thought of as tall and handsome or pretty, although they may be.

However, each one of us can be delicate and adorable when we display inward delicacy. Jesus Christ can make us a humble Apollo. That which is amiable is adorable; that which is graceful is colorful. God can add to his creation landscaping beauty. Jesus Christ was and is our divine Savior, while he was also human. Of the humanistic aspect of his countenance we know very little. However, in Solomon's painting of Jesus, it seems he was concerned about painting what he thought the Master best presented. In his work of art, we see a perfect tableau bringing out perfection in the way one would expect. The Bible speaks about the radiance of Christ, his garments white as snow. Of course the bottom line is our Lord can make, in one sense, all of us attractive.

HE WAS HUMBLE

In Athens, during the memorial service exercised by his young friends, the leader lifted up what to me was Tom III's best characteristic: he was a very humble young man. He

James Thomas Christie III

was not spoiled, although he had so many advantages.

To Tom Christie III, if someone did look upon him as intelligent and handsome, he responded with humility. In his short life, he was already a worldwide traveler. He took on little simple jobs, and, abroad, I'm sure his humility could be noted.

Following his untimely passing from mortality to immortality, if he could have observed such a large gathering of people who paid tribute to his life in his memorial service, it would have astounded him.

An illustration comes to my mind about some children in his congregation's recreational program. Someone questioned if they were properly chaperoned. A reply merged, "Tom Christie III is down there. You don't have to worry." When older youngsters direct their attention to children, you can credit that concerned modesty. When Tom III wrote a thank you note responding to his high school graduation gift in 1983, (which I still have), he stated, "Thank you for the money and especially such a large sum." This noted his docile disposition. I was amazed how he considered an average small gift to represent a large sum.

TOM III—A TRIBUTE

The idea of a tribute to Tom III was conceived in 1990 by the alumni council of the Brookstone High School in Columbus, Georgia. The fundraising was led by Susan Whitaker Covington, a classmate of Tom Christie III.

The work, a painting, is mounted in the foyer at the entrance to the Turner Arts Center on the campus of the Brookstone High School. The portrait hangs on the right, upon entrance to the lobby. It is the only picture in the lobby upon approaching the rotunda.

The profile depicts many cultural qualities. The material emphasizes the photo of a young man seemingly penetrating

LIVING WITH LOSS

Please Join the Family and Friends of
Tom Christie, III
for the Unveiling and Dedication of
Bo Bartlett's
Something About Knowing
Sunday, October 14, 1990
Brookstone School

Turner Arts Center   2:00 P.M.

the unknown. The character involved is arranged with the back of the body to the viewer. The figure is shown with feet slightly lifted, somewhat airborne toward the skies, with a bank of trees distantly beyond. The figure is leaning upward seemingly toward a well-known destiny. The work by the gifted artist Bo Bartlett is dedicated to a graduate of his alma mater.

If Tom Christie III had knowledge today that something so eloquent and complimentary was mounted in such a conspicuous position and dedicated to his memory it would bring him to his knees. I can easily imagine his surprise and most of all his humbleness.

In life as a teenager, Bartlett, the now noted artist, was on a school bus to Brookstone school. A young father, Tom Christie Jr., was placing his son Tom III on the bus. The little boy was enroute to join the first preschool class to be held on the Brookstone Campus. The father looked at Bartlett, then

James Thomas Christie III

a high school student. He placed his child's hand into the hand of the student and said, "Take care of my little boy." During the work of the artist's remarkable mind in the development of his endeavor, he is said to have remarked, "If I could just hold the little boy's hand one more time."

In closing this chapter which I have been so honored to write, I want to share the following note I handed to the officiating minister and thus was read by the pastor during the memorial service.

BRIEF TRIBUTE OF JAMES THOMAS CHRISTIE III

On November 13, 1965, the miracle of birth transpired through Tom Jr. and Joyce Christie. God laid into their hands his most precious gift, a child. In their prudence they chose to call him James Thomas Christie III.

From the time this child began to behold the beauty of this world, he observed, through his parents, desirable precepts and examples. He felt love, envisioned character and stability.

Soon, during his infant days, his mother and father took him to the temple. There he was baptized into the Christian faith on May 15, 1966. Later, at the age of accountability, he chose to confirm into the fellowship of the Church on April 3, 1977.

This lad continued to respond to the noble teachings to which he had been exposed. He passed through youth and adulthood and began himself to reflect faith and character, complimentary qualities.

Through high school, college, and daily life, Tom made use of three powerful, small words, namely, "I love you." This was his typical way of closing a conversation. Moreover, when he placed his strong arms around you, leaving the touch of his lips upon your cheek, it was always "I love you."

LIVING WITH LOSS

In this hour when this prince of a young man is no longer with us in the temporal body, we his family are crushed, something which has happened to others. Yet his memory, his short span of life, twenty-two years, has left us something which is better than gold and silver, more precious than rubies and diamonds. Such memories do not haunt us, they help make us. Tom's warm personality and radiant spirit, though absent in earthly tabernacle, live on. His soul we commend to God.

The gratitude to all who have been so helpful and continue to be, endows us his family, with an obligation we shall respect.

By Tom's Grandfather Veal

CHAPTER TWO

Joyce Veal Christie

ALMOST ALL PEOPLE AT SOME TIME HAVE HEARD THE COMMENT, "When he or she walks in, his or her presence lights up the room." That gift was one of Joyce Christie's attributes. In other words *a notable presence.*

I have not known a person blessed with such endowment who used that gift and luster purposely as a dominating force. People who are equipped with a measure of this nature seemingly know how (and prefer to keep) their house in order. Cutting through some things just because she possessed those prevailing features was the farthest intent from Joyce Christie's mind. Her quality of extension was demonstrated involuntarily. Over and over again, if she possessed any quality characteristics, they were to glorify God. If there were any attributes which sparkled or danced for her, such gifts were to be purposed to God's glorification and never on the wings of some sinister use or personal advantage.

If her presence did draw attention, it was never intentional. Like many people, she possessed an asset which made it possible for her to be comfortable at home or abroad. She was so engaged in noticing and being vocally

LIVING WITH LOSS

complimentary in what she saw in others, she had no time to think of herself as being the center of attention. Her intent was always in regard to her responsibilities and duties, and she never failed to show up and certainly never to show off. Kind friends and neighbors did notice her presence and gifts and openly said so—yes, enough to spoil her. But that was not likely to happen since what she had been taught was so implanted in her heart through the spirit of Jesus Christ.

If any thought had ever entered her mind to permeate and overspread herself for personal advantages, she would have exclaimed, "Satan, get behind me," and in that position she would have been dominating and arrogant. She would have put together a profound presence in the glory of God.

What I have just implied about one's presence is a condition very troublesome in losing our loved ones in death. This hunger and thirst for a family member to arrive again is alive even as we try to accept, and often do, our loved one's soul and spirit having returned to the God who gave it. Yet we cannot avoid thinking about how joyful their presence would be once again. Among God's people today, communities are filled with members of society who miss the steps of a departed loved one that once sounded at the door.

At this moment, it is true there are mothers and fathers who have lost the child whose toe taps they once heard. The footsteps they yearn to hear again. Likewise, the door which once permitted a spouse to enter after a day's toil does not swing open for that special moment anymore. The absence of one's beloved is painful. Parents of a child lost in war, aircraft accident, or otherwise do not have the helpful presence of the body which did not return.

The person I write about here, in former years, after driving up in the backyard, turning off the motor,

Joyce Veal Christie

descending from the auto, and frequently bearing a gift for her parents doesn't appear anymore.

Yes, we all share the notable absence of our child. Our loved ones may not have had the romantic physique and personality to light up the room when appearing in public, but no matter if they were a little dull in life, they turned on the light when they appeared. We can remember, however. We can always feel or sense that presence in spirit, although not in flesh.

This is the omnipresence of Almighty God. The faculties of the mind cause us to sense the whereabouts of one, always there, who can take charge of our labors and our struggles. The creator can help us with the next step. There is always something which makes praise and creates normal peace: "God is our refuge and strength, a very present help in trouble. God is in the midst of her; she shall not be moved; God shall help her and that right early" (Ps. 46:1 and 5).

JOYCE CHRISTIE—THE CHILD

On January 31, 1939, a twenty-two-year-old wife on the verge of bringing into the world her firstborn had returned to the farm home of her parents, Hudson and Susie Brantley. Her decision was odd compared to modern day society, but Lucile had made a decision not uncommon in that day.

Precisely, an expectant mother, prior to the birth of her child, was returning to her parents' home for the greatest, most exciting event of her life.

I suspect that anticipation has been true of almost every mother in history. In Lucile's plans there was no insurance, no hospitalization arrangement, no washing machine, no throw-away diapers. How different it is today. Economical prosperity has propelled us into such an orbit of paradise, and we are grateful.

LIVING WITH LOSS

Great economic progress was taking place while Franklin D. Roosevelt was president of the United States. The hour for the birth of Joyce Veal was on the threshold of the president's birthday. The expectant father was very fond of the president. In his mind there was the thought that hopefully the child would be born on the president's birthday; the possibility was very likely. The period involved was the closing chapter of the Great Depression. Also, it was on the threshold of the monumental World War II.

On January 30, the soon-to-be mother had set up the place of her child's birth to occur in her parents' living quarters; in the part where two double beds were mounted in one of three bedrooms arranged in the wood frame residence. The birth, however, did not occur on the president's birthday.

Two years previously on a Sunday, prior to sunset, a serious decision had been determined between the two of us. We had come to the conclusion we would take our chance with each other in matrimony. At this point the agreement has lasted for sixty happy, rugged, and victorious years. Neither one of us possessed a watch that Sunday evening. The sun was sinking low, and we both knew I soon would be making my departure. Family affairs were in great contrast in those days compared to contemporary. Mrs. Brantley, a noble person of character and culture, had some curfews, mostly about five hours before midnight.

As the evening shadows began to fall across the yard, I asked Lucile to find her father and enquire if I could speak to him. The two of us met on the large front porch. He knew perhaps what I had in mind, and I didn't keep him waiting. Soon he heard a young man's shaky voice explaining to him I wanted to become the husband of his daughter. He in turn made the comment, "If you think you can take care of her, alright."

Joyce Veal Christie

As my mind goes back, my level of maturity at that time would not necessarily register any high mark. Nevertheless, today I feel very good I had enough prudence to copy some old-fashioned character. It makes me proud; at least my behavior in 1937 represented respect and decent consideration. I entered a house I did not build, penetrated into a family I did not raise, and asked for a priceless possession. I had not earned a trophy for which I had not labored. The nature of my course considering Mr. Brantley's appearance was not necessarily the norm or order of that day and certainly not of this day, and I'm not saying it should be.

Today as I look back, there must have been a tad of good in me through asking for the hand of my wife. I'm proud I did and perhaps my course proved some measure of meritoriousness.

In that era, the practice of wedding performance consisted primarily in the office of the justice of peace, probate judge, or magistrate—not for lack of religion, but largely influenced by such circumstances as travel, economy, availability of ministers, and other obstacles.

Bear me one illustration. Recently I enjoyed the following information: Cecil Tharpe, my first cousin, shared with me how his and Sybil's wedding occurred. Mr. Anderson, the justice of peace, was to appear at the bride's residence and officiate. The justice of peace was late. Cecil and Sybil grew anxious because of the delay. Together they drove toward Mr. Anderson's residence. En route they met him, whereupon the couple immediately became man and wife in the middle of the dirt road. Their license document was purchased for three dollars Cecil had borrowed from a cousin. The couple is not financially wealthy, but I can say well in order in monetary and religious aspect.

Church weddings were not heard about in my community during the twenties and thirties. By the same token,

Living with Loss

neither were marriage disailment and separation heard about. I can recall only one case in which the wedding vows were dissolved. That's correct, only one!

Although the presence of a minister was not the norm, Lucile and I sought a clergyman. The ceremony transpired in the Methodist parsonage in Kite, Georgia, performed by the Reverend Doster Vincent, D.D. You see, it was the first wedding I ever saw, yet I was in it; I was intoxicated with love, ecstatic to be sure. It has lasted more than sixty years, but that is not something to boast about. Only through the grace of God could it happen.

I was selfish in giving our children identification for inhabitation upon this planet. I much desired the child to be known as Joyce, a popular name in the thirties. My wife agreed, and so it was. Maybe I was correct, considering the joy Joyce laid upon us while on this earth, just as you once cherished your child until the angels came and hoisted your precious one into a heavenly journey.

So it came to pass on that winter evening, January 30, 1939, Dr. Gordon Brantley, a legend in his home county, showed up. Like other attending physicians in the 1930s, while waiting on a birth, Dr. Brantley mounted a bed for rest and sleep.

A little later a new day had dawned. It was about 2:00 A.M. when our child was only a few minutes away. Multitudes of mothers here and there were experiencing the same discomfort yet the same ultimate joy. The president's birthday had passed, but not the glory of the night. A child whose life ultimately had only one focus—to glorify God—was arriving. A fire sparked in the bedroom for heat and also for light. A nearby wood stove provided warm

Joyce Veal Christie

water if needed. Then the event which many women the whole wide world over can recall transpired for Lucile.

The struggle ceased; another infant—God's great miracle and mankind's most precious gift—was ushered upon the planet. A soul like many other souls born on that day had been placed in orbit.

Have you ever taken an account of what you first noted about the first child you ever saw which you could call your own, yet which ultimately belonged to God?

In the early biological process in any child, one can soon pick up evidence of certain God-given talents and gifts. Such blessings are soon noticed in academic areas, athletic ability, craftsmanship, and technical I.Q. Gifts are noticeable in personality and mannerisms.

The most immediate up-front quality for Joyce was in musical notation. Almighty God arranged through her voice and instrumental use of hands a special talent. The intonation of voice, lungs, modulation, and other gifts were present.

Thus her childhood included from the outset musical talent. At the age of two, she began to entertain others. Our method of travel during her life as a child included my father's automobile. Then there were other methods, including the animal family and horse species. When Joyce was small, travel included a flatbed body, known today as a pick-up, known in that day as one might suspect, the wagon facility.

Yes, in the two-mule-drawn wagon there were times when the group of riders would ask Joyce, then little more than two years old, to sit in the front of the wagon body and sing, "Bye old Baby Bunkin. Daddy's gone a hunting to catch a rabbit skin to wrap the baby up in," or "Jesus loves me this I know. For the Bible tells me so." We had a ball!

In that decade, the clouds of war were heavy and bothersome. Someone had penned some lyrics relating to the conflict. Joyce's mother was surprised when Joyce came into the kitchen singing, "Coming in on a wing and a prayer," at the age of two or three. What made it so surprising was we had no radio, and television was unknown. Thus, "Where had the child heard the tune and words?"

JOYCE—THE YOUNG WOMAN

Joyce's melodic voice at an early age became a useful resource prior to her formal training. Like all grandfathers, hers took pride in his grandchildren. Tom Veal, her grandfather, in his last days preceding death, requested his thirteen-year-old granddaughter do solo work in his funeral celebration. The practice of solos or duets was a standard in funerals. His granddaughter, Joyce, did not hesitate. She sang "Beyond the Sunset" very willingly and effectively at his funeral.

Another contribution she made to many families while in high school and while tutoring at a nearby college transpired through deaths. During a juncture of movements in a rural area while I was officiating for funerals in my own denominations, and also for other Christian fellowships who did not have a pastor, usually the minister was asked to provide vocal music. Frequently, I turned to Joyce; there was never any hesitancy. There was always in her life an innate unexpressed attitude toward glorifying God. It was her secret.

Her formal training began to bear fruition when she enrolled at Wesleyan College in Macon, Georgia, a school noted for its contribution in fine arts. There she toured with the Glee Club and was a participant among seven of the students with the most endowed voices—"The Wesleyans."

As a young mother in Columbus, Georgia, she was one of twelve young matrons who developed what was called

Joyce Veal Christie

"Soft Tones of Faith." In their day, they appeared on television when it was a rare event for any group to be invited for appearance on live T.V. programs. In fact, T.V. stations were sparse. "The Soft Tones of Faith" also developed recordings.

I appeared in worship in my daughter's congregation the day before her funeral service. I sat near the chancel. In conversation with Sis Wood, a close friend of my daughter, the element of music came into play. I mentioned to her, out of all Joyce's musical renditions, (since I was not into electronics), I had never recorded one single measure. God works in mysterious ways, and Mrs. Wood informed me, "Your daughter did the solo work in my wedding, here in this church, and I have the tape of the music."

That led to others coming forth with numerous recordings. Joyce was one of those fortunate individuals blessed in double measure both vocally and instrumentally. The keyboard was perhaps her first love. In early life, a friend, Mrs. Revere, asked her to play the instrument in the funeral of her husband. Joyce confided in her mother, asking her for help. She was nervous and uncomfortable. Therefore, she persuaded her mother to remain on the piano bench beside her.

Some of you may remember when your child made a contribution and helped others while very young, musically or otherwise. You, too, may have lost through death the same child whose talents you once enjoyed.

As she pursued piano training at an early age, an instrument was a must. Since time began, fathers and mothers have labored providing basic needs of their children first. Her need of an instrument challenged us. Dr. Knight loaned us money, and we were happy when Joyce received her piano. She didn't have to be pushed, just given a chance.

Years later, when she was facing death, the two of us were alone together one day talking, as you have done,

LIVING WITH LOSS

with loved ones. In that conversation she stated, "The only thing I regret about my life is I stopped playing the piano." She never lost the touch and performed occasionally. What she meant was she did not maintain practice and learning.

As I have suggested earlier, parents are wise in keeping some records about their children from the time they arrive in the family until they venture forth in their own world. Such memories can be very rewarding down the long road. Mamas and daddies miss opportunities if, for instance, they expend much time and expense on books and albums related to persons of fame and never compile any archives of transcripts of their own children who are always famous to them. This can be done without the necessity of a detailed diary, just periodic script or a log will do.

I kept a copy of my daughter's high school music recital program, April 12, 1957. There were diverse selections including Selfegritte, Bach, Clare de Lune, and Debussy, also, "Wedding of the Painted Doll" and "Moonlight and Roses," which she presented from the Xylophone. On the back page of the program I observed my writing which stated, "Keep this copy." This exact event will never occur again.

The United Methodist Church at one time had the largest printing facility in the world located in Nashville, Tennessee, covering eleven acres of land. The enterprise did contract work for other denominations as well. One of the projects it produced for worldwide service was printing church bulletin formats, a four-page arrangement.

Where I was a pastor in the 1960s, our church bulletins came six weeks in advance for Sunday's preparation. At one

Joyce Veal Christie

time the church secretary left a copy on my desk. The front page format featured the four-level keyboard for one of the largest organs in the world. The photo was taken at Wesleyan College school of liberal and fine arts in Macon, Georgia. Not many, if any, church structures could house the installments. The monumental organ facility was a gift from Mr. Candler, for whom the famous drink of Coca-Cola became such a success worldwide. On the front cover at the console was a charming display of a student. She was a brunette, shown with her arms extended for operation control. The person was attired in a white dress. The picture was very sharp. A ring showed clearly on the person's finger. One could almost determine the time of day from the watch on the wrist. The church secretary had pinned a note on the Sunday bulletin and left it on my desk. It read, "This is your daughter." Joyce came home from school that weekend. You can imagine her consternation on Sunday morning when she received that church bulletin without any previous notice about the cover format.

You know how we parents whoop about our children, who may not appeal to others, but glitter up or down for us. I don't remember the bulletin being discussed with any intent, and I doubt if Joyce kept a copy. It was not that big a deal. What I do know, she had a desirable characteristic which many people have and I seek daily for myself. She had pride on a Godly level of self esteem and self respect. In the meantime, conceit or laudation was no part of her thoughts. I suppose in choosing Scripture for her funeral celebration, that's why she chose 1 Corinthians 13:4–5. "Charity envieth not, vaunteth not itself, is not puffed up, does not behave unseemingly, seeketh not her own." Pride, yes normal pride, is desirable. I join with the mass of Americans who take pride in this great country; citizens of other nationalities do likewise at a level of self-importance as opposed to undesirable ego.

LIVING WITH LOSS

In the final chapter of Joyce's life, she had written a biography of her life. It is brief, probably because it was penned during her illness, and her body was weaker. As you will note later, she herself had noted in reference to the church bulletin photo. The church bulletin read on the front cover:

Great is the Lord and greatly to be praised (Ps. 145:3).

For her life and anything, these word were imminent. Not until then had I noticed how those words described the attitude of the person pictured. For her the main thought of her life included, "To God be the Glory" (Matt. 5:16).

For your child or my child, the vocation they choose in life first of all should never be founded in regard to social level or monetary degree, although interest and encouragement in that direction is acceptable. The immediate consideration should be grounded in how one's earthly pilgrimage contributes to the whole of a republic and God's family.

Although I never pursued playing an instrument, I wish I had. I do enjoy having the dance instinct. My father could do the shuffle quietly and smoothly as silk without any musical assistance. In late life I have developed what he exposed to me, a bit of amateur tap.

Strangely enough, it was about music that my daughter and I experienced some element of clash. Not many parents have ever raised a child from infancy to adulthood and avoided some adversity when their children were considering the matter of higher education, the choice of college.

The parents of the person herein mentioned, gunning for the talented individual to become exposed to the highest quality of training available, were pushing in that direction.

The daughter had another idea. Ten miles from the residence stood a school from which her father graduated. Her

Joyce Veal Christie

potential interest in enrollment at the school was festered in being close to a quality young man in the same county. The parents kept pushing for instruction offering melodious opportunities in music at Wesleyan College. The difference in opinion and preference kept cropping up.

Then one day the father heard footsteps in the corridor outside the church office. The minister soon learned the steps were those of his daughter. Joyce entered the room, pulled up a chair, and preceded to sit down on the opposite side of the desk. I could detect a gift she possessed—namely to take charge where she felt strongly and at the same time be diplomatic. In other words, take charge without charging. In that particular instant she was prepared to offer a strong position according to her own maturity. Her lovely yet stern countenance is today firmly registered in my mental reflexes.

Across the desk, our eyes met, and leaning forward she expressed her purpose. She ventured, "Daddy you can't make me go to Wesleyan College." I answered like a flash. I answered emphatically with three words, "I know it!" Maybe the good Lord had prepared me. Can you believe the subject never came up again? The daughter proceeded to what her parents suggested and which turned out to be, beyond a shadow of a doubt, God's plan for her and all concerned. I cherished her visit. She taught me of my own persistence, which characteristic-wise was perhaps cropping up in other confrontations, even in my own ministry.

While on that line of thought, I must say that Joyce was the best critic I ever had. That's saying much, as my wife has been very constructive. Many people have that gift of charging without charging. Yes, over the years she was my best critic. Something I will always miss.

The following page is an illustration of a letter her parents received from college. There is a statement in which the final lines inspire me more than anything ever said to "my wife and me." I don't believe you will mind reading Joyce's letter word for word, written May 21, 1961.

LIVING WITH LOSS

Above are four illustrations of Joyce's letter to her parents from college. The letter in its entirety is as follows.

Joyce Veal Christie

May 21, 1961

Dearest Folks,

I know you think I've forgotten you, but honestly, I am so busy I have studied all week-end.

I sang at Cherokee Heights this morning at S.S. and then went to Mulberry to church, and thoroughly enjoyed it. I went to church alone, just can't seem to get these girls to go.

The glee-club went to Lake Sinclair yesterday. We had a grand time and I got lots of sun. I had a nice surprise when I got back. Mrs. Harrison, bless her sweet heart, had sent me 5 dresses and told me to choose 3 of them. I'm having a hard time because I love them all and they all fit.

Had a very nice letter from Bro. Hearn yesterday. You must read it.

The girl I was telling you about in the car accident in N.C. died yesterday. I've been rather upset about it although I didn't know her very well. Couldn't even sleep last night and wanted to call you, but didn't.

Haven't dated anyone new lately, but at least some new boys have been calling me and I feel very flattered. Have a date with B. Lloyd tonight, although I don't have time to go out.

Sarah, Lois, and Ovid brought me out here last Sunday from the Macon Hospital. Was very glad to see Ovid. He gave Sarah a mink stole for Mother's Day. Isn't that something!! Wish I could do the same.

Mother, please send me Katie Williams address again. I threw the letter away before I had time to write her.

Hate to mention the subject, but I am truly broke. We had to pay $5.00 Thursday for our caps and gowns and I borrowed that from Bryd. We get $2.50 back after graduation. Also the $10.00 graduation fee cannot be transferred from the $10.00 breakage fee. We get the breakage fee back after graduation and the graduation fee has to be paid in the near future. I can't see the point, but that's the way this school operates. Everyone is disgusted about this because no one has any money. I also have to have a little bit of money for this tea that Flo and I are giving for Sandra. Believe me, I hate to ask you for this, but I see no alternative. Sincerely hope I can make it up to you someday—you have been so wonderful to me—

I have so much work to do, so I'll close—

Please think of me in your prayers, that I may be a more Christian person.

Love you all,
Joyce

P.S. Mother, I meant for Angela to have that notebook. Just save the papers.

P.S.S. Mr. McLean has given me a sterling silver ashtray for graduation. I'm a very lucky girl and I don't feel like I deserve it—Please don't try to get me anything for graduation. You have given me so much already—More than I can ever thank you for—All I want is for you to be here—

Bear with me one brief footnote regarding the letter I did not let get away.

While giving a baccalaureate sermon in 1966 I challenged some soon-to-be college students about their future. Said I, "You are going away from home; this means your parents will not be there. You will be more responsible for your decisions. The state patrol will keep you in line on the highway. The school will make guidelines you must follow.

"The one time you must make a choice is on Sunday morning at 10:00 A.M. You will be on the spot. That moment will be your most challenging test.

"There are no scheduled classes for the day. Every move you make is on a voluntary basis. You are free to choose. The hour is 10:00 A.M. Sunday morning you find yourself in Freedom Hall dormitory.

"Next door and across the corridor, Amon and Manuel have already made a decision. Their footsteps can be heard outside. Their supplies, which include beer, perhaps a six pack, are fixed. They are headed to the park or beach for the day.

Joyce Veal Christie

"There are others, however, through choice, that have announced their destination. They have chosen a special place of gratitude and worship; the church, the synagogue, or whatever. Later they invest their time in some kind of servitude for good."

In the 1960s students had fewer cars. I suspect the numbers of students owning vehicles was minor. Joyce never had any personal transportation in college. She went alone into churches for music ministries where she was not known. Her spiritual maturity was inspiring. She was always perfectly attired. Mrs. Essie Harrison, a parishioner in my congregation in Millen, Georgia, owned and operated a quality ladies dress shop. We have not forgotten her generosity. Also in the sixties, students at Wesleyan wore hats and white gloves off campus.

I love this period of leisure garments. However, lowering the standard of culture and formality has in some measure, perhaps, contributed to weakening our morals and ethics.

Like you, we would have welcomed reasonable suggestions concerning a graduation gift. Joyce deserved something like your daughter or son. I'm sure we did something, nevertheless Joyce had one suggestion, a request, a big deal to her. What she desired more than anything in the world was something affordable for any parent. She wrote:

"Please don't try to get me anything for graduation, you have given me so much already. More than I can ever thank you for. All I want is for you to be there."

ILLNESS

Human suffering has become so widespread on the threshold of a new century. We are all confronted with daily detriments. However, let us not despair. Efforts to reduce our sores are often meeting with success.

Living with Loss

One of the prevailing diseases causing problems with our health is cancer, causing the functioning of our bodies to get off track. The disease has the power to infest our physical creation and dominate and influence our normal welfare. Cancer, the infirmity of the body about which I heard only occasionally long years ago, has become a household word today.

In the spring of 1993, we learned of our daughter's health prognosis. Soon her doctor set up an appointment of special examination at Duke University in Durham, North Carolina. Joyce, like other individuals, preferred to meet her problem as far as she could without involving other people. When the time came to drive the six to seven hundred miles scheduled, she agreed for someone to travel with her, but she opted to do her own driving. We waited at home, experiencing the excruciating suspense of waiting while some medical doctor reports his findings about our bodies, or our loved ones.

On the evening she returned home in March 1993, due to circumstances, we could not speak with our daughter until 10:00 P.M. for a report or diagnosis entailing the spot which developed upon the back of her body. We had no reason to think anything except there needed to be attention to the problem, and, thus, her health would improve. On the contrary, the answers we anticipated were not the answers we received. Although we had been realistic, we were aware our optimism might not parallel reality.

At 10:00 P.M. Joyce was troubled, of course, but not noticeably. "Daddy, the condition has penetrated into the blood stream," was, of course, gloomy information. However, her attitude was upbeat. The physician reported also that such conditions had a healing record of only thirty-three percent. I'm of the opinion she fell asleep late that evening. At least I hope so. Meanwhile, her parents tossed through a restless night as parents often do.

Joyce Veal Christie

Joyce was still wrestling with the death of her only son, which happened in a way requiring unusual stamina and adjustment. Now another period of uphill struggle had come upon the Christie household.

As mentioned earlier, the family (as was in the case of Tom Christie III's death) was immediately surrounded by friends. All of us know how uplifting such spiritual underpinning can be. To be sure, we all know how we depend on each other in responding to needs. When hard things happen to us, immediately, help is on the way.

Remember after the doctor's assistant has seen you and after completing certain attention in leaving the room, you hear the remark, "The doctor will be here in a few minutes." The airline stewardess comments, "Folks, we'll soon be on the ground." The person at the switchboard suggests, "Hold on, help is on the way." The police officer when in need of help in carrying out an assignment, or when in trouble, knows help is on the way.

Ever heard the comment, "I knew you would come?" If there was trouble at the Christie residence, there would be so many on their way, enough to make you cry with gratitude. Know what I mean? Through people, God supports us, directly or indirectly. In the book of Numbers, Moses was overcome with great burden about his people. Moses took his case to God as he spoke, "I am not able to bear all the burden alone because it is too heavy for me" (Num. 11:14). In verse 23 God assured Moses his hand had not waxed short. His needs were met.

When Joyce's illness occurred, we were amazed for the second time how her husband and friends went all out taking care; every need was met, including out-of-state referrals. At times she was flown by jet when no one was aboard but the two pilots, Joyce, and her husband.

Like other cancer patients, she knew of the serious circumstances, yet her faith burned like a candle. Although her recovery was not expected, her gratifying spiritual outlook was so energizing and uplifting.

The oldest daughter preferred to come home long before her mother's death occurred, not that she was needed as far as chores were concerned. Rather, Brantley yearned to practice the highest level of communion with the mother she adored. She took a leave of absence from her office to make it possible.

In the garden located in the rear of the residence, during her mother's illness, our granddaughter and her grandparents were in the residential garden alone. Brantley, with her head in a normal position, spoke as candidly as anyone can. This young adult stated, "You know God must like our family."

From that verbal expression of maturity, isn't it reasonable to accept that God Almighty was pleased?

Jesus Christ had something to say along that line. "He that sent me is with me: The Father hath not left me alone, for I do always those things that please him" (John 8:29).

When the burdens on our hearts become so profound, our best way out is leave the things we cannot change to the care of our Heavenly Father. One must acknowledge a recommendation of this caliber is more easily preached than practiced. Actually the statement by Brantley in the garden pleased God. Think of the other side of the coin where rebellion sets up, and the results are completely opposite.

In Matthew 3:17, we read God's feelings, "This is my beloved son in whom I am well pleased." My granddaughter's faith pleased me. Our Lord was always anxious about what God's children thought of him. The time he was most disappointed was not when someone lashed physical stripes across his back, but his major concern lay in the scope of one's faith. In Hebrews 11:6, Paul wrote, "Without faith it is impossible to please God."

The time he was most disappointed was not when someone did not believe in or accept him as Messiah. When

Joyce Veal Christie

Brantley acclaimed the affirmation, "God must like this family," she pleased God. This is what happens to us as we yield ourselves unto Almighty God. Joy and peace then unite in love. Jesus sought to please his Heavenly Father and did. This tells us how he could suffer so much and yet suffer so little.

I do not know a better prescription to maintain our balance and equilibrium than the well-known proposition about life, which many have stated and used: We must be able to cry a little, and laugh a little. Of course, we all agree in our daily labors we must use a little of this and a little of that. However, at the same time we must make sure we include not a mini status of prayer, but rather a bundle of prayer. In 1 Thessalonians 5:17, 21–22, while St. Paul was naming qualities of the soul, he counseled us as follows: "Pray without ceasing. In everything give thanks: Hold fast to that which is good, abstain from all appearance of evil."

Prayer may not bring to pass every preference and desire of our hopes, but it does render everything best for us. Supplication unto God is healthy spiritual therapy for any living soul.

In 1941, a little cattle-farm house stood on an elevated level of topography. The small residence was surrounded by a beautiful pine forest. The nearest neighbors were about a half mile to the west and one mile east on a dirt road. Homes did not include electric lights or running water.

Four persons inhabited the wood frame structure; Ernest, Lucile, Joyce, and Tommy Veal. The center of the residence offered a large room—space for two double beds.

Living with Loss

The father used one in the evening as he and one small child (Joyce) passed through the night. The mother and a small boy occupied the second bed. All of my life, as a father in the home and otherwise, I had heard and viewed spiritual emphasis, faith, repentance, baptism, and salvation.

In the closing chapter of one particular day at bedtime, the mother of the children spent some time kneeling on the wood floor in communion with God. In that facility, inadequate yet certainly appreciated, a fire crackled in the fireplace, the blaze fading for the evening. My thoughts caused me to do as the mother did; I also knelt on the bare floor beside my bed. In our home, Lucile had never seen me on my knees before. At that point my wife noticed my need. Lucile moved across the room. There she knelt and held me in her arms while the Great Physician operated on my soul. During that memorable evening, a husband and father was spiritually redeemed.

Someone wrote the following similar account of a father's conversion:

A Father's Prayer

Last night my little boy confessed to me
Some childish wrong; and, kneeling at my knee,
He prayed with tears: "Dear God, make me a man
Like Daddy, wise and strong—I know You can!"
Then, while he slept, I knelt beside his bed,
Confessed my sins, and prayed with low-bowed head:
"O God, make me a child, like my child here
Pure, guileless, trusting Thee with faith sincere."

Surely God must have known while I was looking into the unknown a distant fifty-six years later I would need to reach back and recall that glorious evening. I would find, in the loss of a child, and in the sleeping child, a power I didn't have. Instead of an evening in a weak residential structure,

Joyce Veal Christie

I slept in a castle with a child whose tender mind went on to glorify God.

You and I thoroughly understand the power of prayer. Almighty God is so powerful. Fifty years ago, few people prayed verbally in open public, and today many hesitate also. Unfortunately there is due fear or discomfort at times. Do you remember the first time you offered prayer aloud in public? I do, and I was uncomfortable and shaky in one sense while, on the other hand, at ease.

In 1943, in what was then Morrison Memorial Methodist Church in Macon, Georgia, Reverend Swoll Sawyer was pastor, and my young family regular participants. In a Wednesday evening prayer service, the Holy Spirit pushed me into open verbal language in spiritual entreaty.

Looking back, I can fully understand how God was preparing the release of my timidity in the rear lines to move forward into the front lines. Soon I was inducted into the military conflict of World War II. In that terrible time, we were losing the war. I was in the company and presence of youth just out of their teens, as well as fathers. These persons were frightened and had an absence of peace and an uncertain future. I was in their midst. I had no office, no rank but seaman third class. Often times I would suggest to those around me that we pause and have impromptu prayer. I had no credentials or plans. I was speaking to people who welcomed anyone who could offer a prayer in the presence of other people. As in any situation, many of the servicemen in groups were pesky and tough going, yet I was never rebuked, but rather always respected. Any subject which can bring practically everyone to silence and respect, like the word prayer, is within itself living proof. God Is!

Something happened during that gigantic international battle, which to me represents an act of prayerful valor more than any illustration I know about. Such gallantry would be hard to exceed. When the information

LIVING WITH LOSS

first came to me, my response was, "Are you sure?"

In 1945 the U.S. transport ship *Dorchester*, crowded to capacity with our military personnel, was sighted by the enemy. The transport vessel was soon under attack and, for most part, helpless in defense of the onslaught of torpedoes.

On that powerful water vehicle were four chaplains who were not forced to be there. The dedication of the clergy has always produced as many ministers as needed during war. In some instances, over the years, clergymen have been disappointed they could not qualify and, thus, not be accepted in the perilous times of conflict. Moses and Aaron, at the direction of God, selecting personnel from the twelve tribes of Judah, were excused. The priestly group among the Israelites was not drafted. Our government has never forced the clergy into war. This cordial respect was originated of God through Moses. On that fateful day, four chaplains surrendered their life jackets to enlisted comrades, while the *Dorchester* was sinking. They were:

> George Fox—Methodist
> Daniel Poling—Reformed
> Alexander Good—Jewish
> Clark Washington—Catholic

The last view of those immortal four showed them going to a watery grave, locked in each other's arms, intoning The Lord's Prayer. They demonstrated the power of prayer unexcelled. At the same time, four mothers somewhere were losing a child. Those mothers somewhere in the U.S. would be sustained through communion with God. What would perhaps be overlooked would be the days and nights to follow, and the hours when the sleep for those distraught parents would come in broken doses. The fathers and mothers of these heroic gentlemen of the cloth

Joyce Veal Christie

would join with others in losing a child at war. Peace for them would often come through periodic moments, yet so frequently through the spiritual entreaty of God; tranquility would flood their souls.

THE SECOND OF THREE WEEKENDS
OCTOBER 2–4, 1993

The date was the second of three, not only heavy, but almost unbearable weekends in the Christie family.

On a Friday in October 1993, my wife and I had departed from Columbus and driven home for a short time. The next day, Saturday, we were updated on the severity of our daughter's condition.

Only a few years earlier on Saturday, October 8, 1988, the mother of our grandson called to share the overwhelming news she and her husband had lost their twenty-two-year-old son. Only five years later, in 1993, we were losing our child, the mother who had already lost a child. Soon we were back in Columbus.

In our hymnody there are hymns where the word holy is so frequently used. The adjective is used to describe a scene of sacredness. Included in these hymns is the expression *holy*, especially employed in the Christmas Yuletide season. For instance, there is "Oh, Holy Night." This arrangement is primarily performed through solo rendition.

There is also a hymn which for some sixty days, November and December, is heard more than any other piece of music: "Silent Night, Holy Night."

Living with Loss

The words were written by Joseph Mohr, a Catholic priest, on December 4, 1848, in Salzsburg, Austria. The lyrics were given to Fran Gruber, another Austrian. The presentation was made to Gruber during an evening program at a little schoolhouse, where Mohr was the teacher. That same night Gruber set the words with the guitar.

Some twenty years ago in my pastorate, there were some young adults who took upon themselves the planning and administration of a church program without my assistance. I was pleased! During the weekend I had prepared for the upcoming Sunday, yet on Saturday night, I wanted to offer my support to the meeting. I expected to leave the gathering early. I didn't realize what was happening would lead to such "a Holy night." The group included members of various Christian denominations and met in the Methodist church and was led by a Catholic layman. The further into the program we moved, the more my attention was claimed.

Near 12 P.M., a lady began her leadership role whereupon she announced, "Folks, I'm your late movie."

There was a rich presence of the Holy Spirit. The movement included salvation identified through people kneeling at the altar. There one could hear quiet sobbing and detect sound of crying. The room was dimmed by reducing the lighting. The hour glorified God. It was a holy night. Up until that time, it was the holiest evening I had ever known. The noise was not much above a whisper. People were embracing each other in the spell of righteousness. It was a holy assembly; the most enviable hour of worship affecting me publicly in my lifetime.

Yet the most sacred evening ever for me transpired at my daughter's residence on Sixteenth Avenue in Columbus, Georgia, on Saturday, October 2, 1993. The scene and transitions were so painful, yet so calm and serene. There were no visitors; the family preferred privacy. Only one non-family person was present. Joyce Christie remained

Joyce Veal Christie

coherent but gravely ill. Her bedroom seemed not to display crushing circumstances, though they were. The high post bed where she rested pointed upward. As someone has said in trying circumstances, the outlook can be dark while the uplook is beautiful. I paced to and fro in front of the residence. God's holy sabbath was approaching. Local traffic was silent. In each neighbor's residence a light burned brightly upfront, silence was profound. Noise had ceased. 'Twas the holiest hour of the holiest for me, ever. It seemed guardian angels were to meet our needs, just as they have performed for others.

Later, at two o' clock in the morning, Sunday, the faint heartbeat failed to go on while the soul gained momentum. The Bible reports on numerous occasions the unique central presence of God. For instance, "God the Lord thy God walketh in the midst of the camp to deliver thee" (Deut. 23:14).

At one point the disciples of Jesus were in deep trouble, then later that day, in the evening when the doors were shut where they were assembled, for fear of the enemy, "Jesus came and stood in their midst, and saith unto them; Peace be with you" (John 20:19). Furthermore, Jesus prayed regarding his own departure for his disciples, "The glory which thou gavest to me I give to them" (John 17:22). So often in death, God is glorified. Joyce could not have the one thing she urgently desired—health. However, the principal thing she wanted most she could have, namely that her life and death glorify God the Father, Son, and Holy Spirit.

That Sunday morning I paused at the door of her bedroom. The angels had taken her away. I did not enter. Was it any wonder? Not ever before had I viewed such a sad, yet glorious scene. A tall stool had been placed close to her high post bed. Perched upon the seat was her daughter, Brantley, as stated previously, who had taken a leave of absence to be with her mother.

LIVING WITH LOSS

In the bedroom a voice broke the silence. My granddaughter, while placing her head near to her mother's head, held a Bible. I could not detect whether she was reading or chanting. Her voice was loud—above conventional level. I could fully absorb I was viewing a memorable scene, yea spiritual acclamation, an immortal hour of "O Holy Night."

I have never discussed that celestial experience with my granddaughter. Surely it was a spiritual gathering of the spirit. I had witnessed a transition where earthly and heavenly met with an immortal hook-up, sealing a chain never to be severed.

Fifty-four beautiful years had passed since January 31, 1939, when I stood near a bed in her Brantley grandparents' residence experiencing what other fathers have felt while a soul was being ushered into the world.

Then on that holy night fifty-four short years later, I stood in Joyce's bedroom, now the mother herself, while her lifeless form was being ushered out of her own stately residence. "The glory of the Lord shined round about." It was now a holy morning. During those days, more than one person said something to me we do not normally hear in times of melancholy: "I know you are a proud father." You who have lost a child can go a long way on precious memories about a life well lived through a son or daughter.

At 8:30 A.M. that same morning, St. Luke Methodist Church had prepared for morning worship. Well did I know, as in other congregations, there one can find abiding support. How could we live without this immortal institution, the church?

The preparation for worship was at its best. Once again, the elements of Holy Communion were waiting to be administered to all who desired. A Holy Night had passed. A Holy Sabbath had dawned. The celebration, the Lord's Supper, was the only time Jesus ever suggested something specifically be

Joyce Veal Christie

done in remembrance of him. Needless to say, a benediction came upon me as a participant.

The liturgy, which normally necessitates attention, would require absolutely no consideration. Joyce Christie saw to that. Every detail had been prepared at its best.

I do not recall viewing the detailed ritual in print until some time following the service. Clergy, while preparing to officiate in funerals, try to give their best in the midst of family distress. When I look upon what my own daughter had prepared relative to her own victory in life, I was taken aback. One can imagine my gratification as a minister while observing something my own child had worked through in complete mental balance in the midst of overwhelming circumstances. Her gallantry has meant more to me than all the books I have ever read, all the material I've ever published.

Her wishes were carried out in detail through her pastor Rev. Marion Edwards, and of laity, Ginger Calhoun. Since that autumn Monday morning, I have used in eulogies the material she highlighted, believing the biblical passages would comfort others in pain from the loss of a child or other loved ones.

ORDER OF WORSHIP

Funeral—Joyce Christie
October 4, 1993
By: Joyce Christie

Prelude   John Miller

Welcome

LIVING WITH LOSS

Call to Worship   2 Timothy 4: 7–8.

I have fought a good fight, I have finished my course, I have kept the faith.

    Henceforth there is laid up for me a crown of righteousness, which the Lord, the righteous judge, shall give me at that day; and not to me only, but unto all them also that love his appearing.

Opening Prayer Reading:
Precious Lord, Take My Hand #474

1. Precious Lord take my hand, lead me on, let me stand,
   I am tired, I am weak, I am worn;
   through the storm, through the night, lead me on to the light;
   Take my hand precious Lord, lead me home.

2. When my way grows drear, precious Lord, linger near.
   When my life is almost gone,
   hear my cry, hear my call, hold my hand lest I fall;
   Take my hand precious Lord, lead me home.

3. When the darkness appears and the night draws near,
   and the day is past and gone,
   At the river I stand, guide my feet, hold my hand;
   Take my hand, precious Lord, lead me home.

Words by Thomas A. Darsey 1932
Music by Thomas A. Darsey 1932

Hymn #77:   How Great Thou Art
                                   Leader Charles Bradley

I. O Lord my God, when I in awesome wonder
    consider all the worlds thy hands have made,

Joyce Veal Christie

I see the stars, I hear the rolling thunder,
Thy power throughout the universe displayed,

Chorus:
Then sings my soul, my Saviour God to thee;
How great thou art, how great thou art!
Then sings my soul, my Saviour God to thee;
How great thou art, how great thou art!

II. When through the woods and forest glades I wander
and hear the birds sing sweetly in the trees;
When I look down from lofty mountain grandeur
and hear the brook and feel the gentle breeze.
(Chorus)

III. And when I think that God his Son not sparing,
sent him to die, I scarce can take it in;
That on the cross, my burden gladly bearing,
he bled and died to take away my sin;
(Chorus)

IV. When Christ shall come with shout of acclamation
and take me home, what joy shall fill my heart.
Then I shall bow in humble adoration,
and there proclaim, my God how great thou art!
(Chorus)

Words: Stuart K. Hine   1953
Music: Stuart K. Hine   1953

Affirmation of Faith: 23rd Psalm

The Lord is my shepherd, I shall not want.
He maketh me to lie down in green pastures:
he leadeth me beside the still waters.
He restoreth my soul: he leadeth me in the paths

Living with Loss

of righteousness for his name's sake.
Yea, though I walk through the valley of the shadow
of death, I will fear no evil:
for thou art with me; thy rod and they staff
they comfort me. Thou preparest a table before me
in the presence of mine enemies:
thou anointest my head with oil; my cup runneth over.
Surely goodness and mercy shall follow me all the days
of my life: and I will dwell in the house of the Lord
forever.

Scripture: 1 Corinthians 13

Though I speak with the tongues of men and of angels,
and have not charity, I am become as sounding brass,
or a tinkling cymbal. And though I have the gift
of prophecy, and understand all mysteries,
and all knowledge; and though I have all faith,
so that I could remove mountains,
and have not charity, I am nothing.
And though I bestow all my goods to feed the poor,
and though I give my body to be burned,
and have not charity, it profiteth me nothing.
Charity suffereth long, and is kind;
charity envieth not; charity vaunteeth not
itself, is not puffed up. Doth not behave itself unseemly,
seeketh not her own, is not easily provoked
thinketh no evil; Rejoiceth not in iniquity
but rejoiceth in the truth; Beareth all things,
believeth all things, hopeth all things,
endureth all things; Charity never faileth:
but whether there be prophecies, they shall fail:
whether there be tongues, they shall cease;
whether there be knowledge, it shall banish away.
For we know in part, and we prophesy in part.
But when that which is perfect is come,
then that which is in part shall be done away.
When I was a child, I spoke as a child,
I understood as a child, I thought as a child:

Joyce Veal Christie

but when I became a man, I put away childish things.
For now we see through a glass, darkly;
but then face to face: now I know in part;
but then shall I know even as also I am known.
And now abideth faith, hope, charity, these three;
but the greatest of these is charity.

Pastoral Prayer and Lord's Prayer.

Our Father which art in heaven, Hallowed by thy name.
Thy kingdom come. Thy will be done in earth as it is in
heaven. Give us this day our daily bread.
And forgive us our trespasses, as we forgive those
who trespass against us. And lead us not
into temptation, but deliver us from evil;
For thine is the kingdom, and the power, and the glory,
Amen.

Scripture Selections

Habakkuk 3: 17–19

Although the fig tree shall not blossom,
neither shall fruit be in the vines;
The labor of the olive shall fail, and the fields shall yield
no meat; the flock shall be cut off from the fold,
and there shall be no herd in the stalls;
Yet I will rejoice in the Lord, I will joy in the God
of my salvation. The Lord God is my strength,
and he will make my feet like hinds' feet,
and he will make me to walk upon high places.

Isaiah 40:29–31

He giveth power to the faint;
and to them that have no might he increaseth strength.
Even the youths shall faint and be weary,
And the young men shall utterly fall;

LIVING WITH LOSS

But they that wait upon the Lord shall renew their
strength;
they shall mount up with wings as eagles;
They shall run, and not be weary;
And they shall walk and not faint.

Romans 8:18, 28, 37–39

For I reckon that the sufferings of this present time
are not worthy to be compared with the glory
which shall be revealed in us.
And we know that all things work together
for good to them that love God,
to them who are the called according to his purpose.

Nay, in all these things we are more
than conquerors through him that loved us.
For I am persuaded that neither death, nor life,
nor angels, nor principalities, nor powers,
nor things present, nor things to come,
Nor height, nor depth, nor any other creature,
shall be able to separate us from the love of God,
Which is in Christ Jesus
our Lord.

St. John 14: 1–6

Let not your heart be troubled: ye believe in God,
believe also in me. In my Father's house
are many mansions; if it were not so,
I would have told you. I go to prepare a place for you.
And if I go and prepare a place for you,
I will come again, and receive you unto myself;
that where I am, there ye may be also.
And whither I go ye know, and the way ye know.
Thomas saith unto him, Lord, we know not
whither thou goest; and how can we know the way?
Jesus saith unto him, I am the way, the truth,
and the life: no man cometh unto the Father, but by me.

Joyce Veal Christie

Meditation

Hymn #480   O Love that Wilt Not Let Me Go
                                    Charles Bradley

1. O love that will not let me go, I rest my
   weary soul in thee; I give thee back the life I owe, that
   in thine ocean depths its flow may richer, fuller be.

2. O Light that followest all my way, I yield my
   flickering torch to thee; my heart restores its borrowed
   ray, that in thy sunshine's blaze
   its day may brighter, fairer be.

3. O Joy that seekest me through pain, I can-not
   close my heart to thee; I trace the rainbow thru the
   rain, and feel the promise is not in vain,
   that man shall tearless be.

4. O Cross that liftest up my head, I dare not
   ask to fly from thee; I lay in dust life's glory dead and
   from the ground there blossoms red life
   that shall end-less be.

Words by George Machurson   1882
Music by Albert Peace   1884

After beginning the writing of this book, a notebook came into my hands.

The material, which I had not seen previously, contained writings by Joyce about her personal life. This entry was

LIVING WITH LOSS

written on June 12, 1993. Her language represented autobiographical information and other oral language explaining her trials and sufferings regarding the loss of a child, which at that time I had never experienced.

I feel comfortable returning to that station in her life and using this material publicly in as much as I spoke with her regarding authorization of setting in motion this publication I have put together.

I have chosen at this point rather than to chop up the material and use periodic inserts, to copy as it is written without proofreading or changes. Her work came from the heart at a time when she was struggling not only with her great loss but also the mental anguish of her illness. In the face of all this, I'm thankful for what she did, and perhaps she would have written more had it not been just four months before her death. One of the best messages was, to me, that she felt God was preparing her and her family to face the future, although tragedy was to follow she would never know about.

June 12, 1993

*I grew up in a Christian home with Godly parents. My daddy is a retired Methodist minister, and I have been in the church all my life. I think I have always had a heart for the Lord and have always had a "partial commitment" to Him. Church has always been very important to me, and I always felt it necessary to be there on Sunday mornings and other occasions. I guess you could say that I was "religious" with being in church and good works being my focus. I loved the Lord and feared Him, but I was unfamiliar with having a relationship with Him. I really thought "being and doing good" was the ticket. I remember when I was in college, my picture playing the organ was on the front of a Methodist bulletin appearing throughout either the conference or the state or whatever. It was quite a surprise to me, and my daddy told me the Lord **really** wanted my heart. That statement made quite an impression on me, and I remember it well.*

Joyce Veal Christie

*I married Tom Christie on June 16, 1963. After 2 years we had a son, James Thomas Christie, III. Two years later we had a daughter, Joyce Brantley Christie. My life was going great! When my children were small I was invited to go to a Bible study, and I began going. The teacher was Barbara Goodrae. I started studying the Bible and learning Scripture. One of the first verses I learned was Ephesians 2: 8,9. What a relief to learn that I didn't **have** to do all those good works anymore, but that my salvation was a gift from God, not based on any performance of my own. Praise the Lord! Another verse I learned about that same time was 1 Corinthians 10: 13 where the Lord says He doesn't give us more than we can bear. This Bible study evolved into another one, and I was taking baby steps as a Christian, I suppose because I didn't have any significant needs.*

Everything was going well, and I was invited to join the "Soft Tones of Faith," a ladies singing group. That was probably the most fun thing I've ever been involved in, and I loved it. We sang, witnessed, and had Bible studies. I loved the Soft Tones, but we disbanded in September 1978. I had just discovered that I was pregnant (what a shock) with Ruth Wilson Christie. I was very upset that I was pregnant, but Tom was elated! God, in His wisdom, gave us the gift of Ruth, because He knew what lay ahead for us. How I praise Him and thank Him for her and my other two children. She was born April 18, 1979 and everything was fine until March 1986 when I was diagnosed with melanoma in my eye. My world came to an end! I could not believe this was happening to me. I was depressed and terrified! Terrified of losing my eye. I hardly thought about the cancer because I was so scared that my eye might be removed.

I was directed and led to the Will Eye Hospital in Philadelphia where my eye was treated with a radiation implant. My eye was saved, and my vision is 20-20. Praise God, that He gave me this restoration. Throughout this time I felt a need for God that I had never felt before. As I walked through the valley, He was my strength and my hope. I drew

Living with Loss

near to Him, and He drew near to me. I think I realized for the first time in my life that nothing else really mattered except God and His word. Family and love are next in order, but God is eternal. I began to see Jesus clearer than I had ever seen Him as I began to really depend on Him because I was in a critical situation.

Feeling my desperate need for Him, I began to go to Precept Bible Study at Edgewood Baptist Church with Ginger Calhoun as the teacher. Wow! I knew I was in the right place the first day. I think joining this Bible Study was the real turning point in my life. I had such a hunger to study the word and get to know the Lord better. The more that was revealed to me, the more I wanted to know. I praise God that He led me to this Bible Study and that it has changed my life. My priorities, my perspective on life, and my destination. God is so good! I made a deeper commitment to Him, and I love Him so. I know now that He was preparing me (as much as I could be prepared) for the next trial in my life.

As my eye had responded and all was well there, I bounced along and did great until October 8, 1988. Brantley called during the night to tell us the worst news that any parent could ever hear. Our son had attempted to take his life. Oh, God, the darkness and pain of that moment! Only the Father could understand! Our world collapsed. Even greater than my own pain was the pain of seeing my precious husband writhing and crying in agony for a son whom he loved more than his own life. Oh Tom, Tom how we love you! That moment in my life is really indescribable; it was so horrible. As friends prepared for us to fly to Athens, I just prayed that God would allow him to live until we got there. I never prayed that he would live because I knew how terrible it was.

The Lord answered my first prayer, and he was still living when we got there. Oh the heartbreak of seeing him as we stroked him and told him how much we loved him. I was almost panicked as I began to look for someone to pray with me. I just prayed that the Lord would send someone. I was standing in

Joyce Veal Christie

the hall and looked up and saw a young man coming down the hall carrying his Bible. I knew the Lord had sent him. It was Mark Magoni, and he and I went in and prayed together with Tom. Oh God is so good! After I felt at peace, I could release him. His daddy and I did release him and asked the Lord to go ahead and take him, and he died. I am thankful for the few short hours we had with him, for the memories of a beautiful life, of a beautiful person so kind, loving, and tender. He was loved by many, and the fruit of his life lives on.

The day after Tom died Kay Arthur came to our house, and my husband received salvation and became a committed Christian. God is so good! Tom's funeral service was beautiful because Jesus was lifted! There were so many people! God truly loved us and carried us through this time through other people. **The pain of losing a child is indescribable as I have said. I felt like my heart had been ripped out, never to be repaired. I felt so empty, so lonely, so sad as I missed Tom and the bright future shared with him shattered and gone.** *Oh Tom, my son, how I love you! The Lord carried me and took me under his wing through Ginger Calhoun. She stayed with me, loving me and encouraging me. I don't know if we could have made it without her. Thank you, Lord for giving her to us. As we plunged into this valley and this darkness, we never lost sight of the light of our Lord. We were just more committed to him.*

Three years after Joyce's death the following paper came into my hands. The article "The Sunset" came about during the high school days of Lindsey Berard. Through the heading, one can note Lindsey was given an assignment through her English teacher, Mrs. Tina Epperson at Brookstone High School, Columbus Georgia.

Living with Loss

The article, "The Sunset," is printed exactly as it was written from the mind and depth of Lindsey's heart and soul.

Pictured above is Lindsey Berard's three-page article "The Sunset." The article reprinted in its entirety follows.

Joyce Veal Christie

Lindsay Berard
Mrs. Epperson
English 11
5 February, 1996

The Sunset

 Anyone who knew Joyce Christie would have to say that she came close to being a perfect person. Joyce is what you would call "A Real southern bell," with that southern drawl she epitomized the southern woman. She was a very loving woman, who always had time for everyone, even to the exclusion of herself. Her gentle manner made her beautiful on the inside as well as the outside. She was a very attractive woman with warm loving eyes, A Terrific smile and a great figure, which I am sure was probably envied by many a mom. Joyce lead us through the hard times, always giving us words of wisdom using the Bible as her inspiration. She was a true Christian living each minute for the Lord. Joyce always tried to make everyone happy by teaching us to love one another.

 Joyce has played a big role in who I am today. From the time I can remember her daughter, Ruth and I have been good friends. She has raised me like one of her own. Her motherly affection extended to all of Ruth's friends. She gladly took us places like swimming lessons, birthday parties, piano lessons, ballet, basketball, the mall, and especially carpool for school. She was our first music teacher, in four year old kindergarten at St. Thomas, she played piano on and taught us songs such as "The Wheels on the Bus" and "Jesus Loves Me". She was more than happy to cook for us, her baked buttered crackers were the best. She even cleaned up after us, but most of all she loved us. She was like our mother.

 In the year 1989, she was diagnosed with cancer. It started as a tumor behind her eye. The cancer was much more serious than our mothers led us to believe. For five years, we watched not knowing the turmoil she was going through. Toward the end as the cancer spread intensely throughout her body, it was difficult to watch this perfect

Living with Loss

southern lady deteriorate into a helpless person. I don't think I ever saw her, when I was a child, stop to rest. It was just so awkward seeing everyone taking care of her; cooking, cleaning, and having to serve her. I was the last one of my friends to see Joyce. She was laying on the couch with a blanket over her; she looked very pale with dark circles under her lifeless looking eyes. The smile that I loved so much and lit up a room was barely there. Her arms that were always there to give me a big hug were to weak to raise. There was at least eight of her friends with her in that room, one of them was my mother. Joyce called me over to where she was and told me what a beautiful young woman I turned out to be and that she was very proud of who I am. You could tell in the way she was smiling, that she was very pleased and proud in how all of "her girls" had turned out. After walking out of the house, I knew that that visit would be the last. I looked through the window to see her for the last time in the house where I spent alot of time and memories. That next week she died, this was the hardest part of it all, letting her go. It all seemed like a bad dream but I was very thankful that I got to tell her that I loved her. I went to be with Joyce for the last time, at her burial in Concord. It is so hard to lose someone who has been a big part of your life and who helped to shape the person that I am today. I never realized how much Ruth was like her mother until the funeral; she was the only one standing tall and strong. That day I was really mad at God for taking such a great person away from us. How could he do that to Ruth? Why would God create such misery? During this time I really began to question my faith.

When my parents and I got up to our river cabin, where we were staying for the weekend. I went to my special spot, the hammock, where I go to think. I sat there for a long time thinking about Joyce and what inspirational word of wisdom she would say. I knew then that she would want me to rejoice and be thankful that I have the Lord in my life to help me through hard times. At that time, the most beautiful sunset appeared in the sky. It was a mixture of

Joyce Veal Christie

the colors orange, red, pink, and purple with the deep orange sun right in the middle, just as if Joyce was telling me how God should be the center of my life. At that point I knew that God was telling me that it was time for Joyce's pain and suffering to end. The sunset made me realize that she wasn't gone, her spirit was still alive in me and it was up to me to do what she always asked and that is to keep God in our heart. I knew at that point that she is living peacefully in heaven and that she is still watching over me. I have since then gone through many deaths and whenever I get depressed I think about Joyce and how God let me know that she would live eternity the way she wanted, in heaven. If it wasn't for the sunset and Joyce's presence I might still be questioning my faith.

Lucile did not share what she had written with me (although I had heard her comment orally earlier) until I had finished this manuscript. With her permission, the story of her vision is as follows:

Three days before Joyce's death, I had the most wonderful vision.

In this vision at an outdoor setting, the emcee said, "We have some young people who are going to tell us about some of their visits." A young man spoke first telling us about some places he had visited in Europe. Then a young lady began to tell some places she had visited abroad. Suddenly I realized those were my grandchildren.

Then the emcee said, "Now we have a person who is going to fly for us. The emcee stood her upon a stool. Immediately she lifted her arms and began to soar toward heaven. When she was airborne, she changed into a beautiful white angel.

Living with Loss

I saw that she was my daughter, Joyce Veal Christie. I believe her spirit left her body that night, and she went to live with our heavenly father. That was the most wonderful experience, seeing my own daughter fly into the arms of our Lord and Saviour, Jesus Christ, to live forever.

CHAPTER THREE

James Thomas Christie Jr.

AS TEENAGERS, MY WIFE AND I WERE ALWAYS INTRIGUED BY athletics. During the age of youth, however, any athletic opportunity for our participation was minute. For one reason equipment was not affordable. In town ball, we managed with a narrow board for a bat.

The crude method also included the use of what was called a Georgia Knit men's sock. This was after the bottom section of the footwear had seen its day. The knitting part of the top could be unraveled and the yarn whipped round and round some material as the center, and the result was a fairly good product for town ball.

Our interest still takes us to high school athletic events. When we were nearing sixty, we had never attended a college football game. However, I knew what it was to be invited to the University of Georgia football game to offer a prayer. I was too busy to go.

In the meantime, there was a young man who knew us well, and we knew him well. He was a graduate of the University of Georgia.

Without previously bringing it up, one evening he lifted from his pocket two tickets for the annual Georgia–Florida

LIVING WITH LOSS

football game. "I want you two people to go," said he. We did, and this was our first college football game.

A few days later the same person repeated the same courtesy. "Here are two tickets for the Sugar Bowl where Georgia will play Arkansas. I want you to go." We did. Also, we often ate in commercial dining places with that same individual and his family. Who would be responsible for the ticket was also forbidden territory. No way Tom Christie Jr. would yield. You see, he was our son-in-law. It is no wonder when we lost him in death we were so broken and still are! Also, his mother had lost her first child in death, her only son.

Many of you out there very intimately know someone who came to your house and, with your approval, collected your child, who in turn bore his name. That young man did not underestimate his blessings. Thus, in response, he spent much of his time and energy trying to prove he did not take for granted what had come his way. Tom Christie Jr. was that kind of son-in-law.

Do you have a son or daughter who had been dating someone you had never met, although you were informed perchance afterwards the relationship would reach the point of likely matrimony? True enough, either the son or daughter informed you a decision had been made and wanted you to meet her fiancé and, later, his parents.

And so it was our daughter, in 1963, informed us her romance with a young man had developed to the level we needed to meet her fiancé, the person with whom she planned to establish a home and family. Our daughter arranged the place and time when we would gather to be in the presence of the man who would be her husband.

In the guest house of the Martin family's elaborate residence in Columbus, Georgia, where Joyce had rented the attractive guest cottage as her apartment, we met. While we had little information about his up-front personality, roots, or mannerisms, what we had been informed about

James Thomas Christie Jr.

his family's background and preparation for life was enough to assure us no hesitancy. To us, he was o.k.

You and I have known of some unfortunate moves by young people regarding marriage. Some unthinkable decisions are made without respect and consideration of parents. For instance, there is sometimes no forewarning to parents when crossing religious lines entailing different faiths or religion; furthermore, the information may not be shared about a fiancé whose character and habits are undesirable, or if the marriage crosses racial lines or national boundaries. Also, there are conditions involving moral questions. This kind of negligence does not always cause problems but certainly runs the risk of causing problems.

Many parents have lost sleep through a child's poor judgement or downright selfishness. In our situation, perhaps like yours, we could place complete trust in our daughter. We had no anxiety, no suspense, only anticipation for a rewarding introduction to Tom Christie Jr., whose life began as an infant in the arms of remarkable parents.

As I look back now, I did not realize God had brought into my life, through my daughter, someone one hundred percent compatible with my particularities. The element of our meeting was a little different to what one might expect in that era. You see, Tom didn't arrive in a sports car or flashy vehicle. Instead he was using a very simple machine. His attire did not include trousers with matching sports jacket and tie. Rather his dress displayed what he liked best: khaki trousers, leisure shoes. Those things, of course, were of little concern to us. We were looking for a person with desirable characteristics. Immediately that concern posed no question.

Tom Christie had not arrived with any thought of impressing someone. He was merely activating his innate natural instincts. That evening a simple-hearted person

Living with Loss

with loving characteristics met a simple-hearted preacher. From the very beginning our symmetrical personalities were pleasantly in tune. Always were!

TOM CHRISTIE—THE SIMPLE MAN

The word "simple" is often misunderstood, offering opportunities, like any other word, for two different meanings and, thus, misunderstanding. In the employment of the language, "simple" in this case by no means suggests a character as rustic or uncompounded. I have just mentioned a simple-to-be son-in-law met a simple-to-be father-in-law.

Over the years people, particularly my parishioners, have labeled me with some terminology one can accept with two different interpretations. Often someone stated, "you are so down to earth." Such terminology could be viewed as being a little short. However, to me, the term is complimentary. An illustration follows.

During the experience of giving eleven sermons in one week in my home church during my infancy in preaching, the following transpired.

After a service outside the building, a person whom I had known all my life made an evaluation of my sermon. He said, "Ernest, we love to hear you preach. We ain't nothing but a bunch of fools out here. We can understand you." Well did I know, the person speaking to me was no simplex but, rather, blessed with an excellent mind, as I had known him all my life. Furthermore, I knew the persons hearing me were no unadornments. They were competent individuals. We all respond to whatever is austere and easy to understand.

Take for instance this age of hi-tech. As much as we appreciate the era of automation, we would upon occasion

James Thomas Christie Jr.

wish we could call a simplifier, someone to unmix the situation. A comment I often make readily is when someone has written a book for children: "That's for me, where can I get a copy?"

Response to simplicity crops up in unbedecked spiritual interest. In the early movements of the church denomination of my ministry, history reports during the primitive age of early Americans, two particular preachers were of diverse disposition. One was envisioned as very austere in sermon delivery, polished indeed! The minister, of course, was effective. However, the other clergyman was viewed as a simple-hearted, loving soul. Of the two, while both contributed, the latter proved more productive, a simple-hearted, loving soul.

What I'm saying about my son-in-law's pure heartedness could be heard in his lightheartedness. Often when I was in his home overnight, as he departed early in the morning for his work and the day, he would lastly speak, "Don't forget to mow the lawn before you leave." If perchance not a son-in-law, there is someone who moves in your circles, who parallels your likeness. Such similitude often becomes blessed attributes in marriage or business and in other relationships.

TOM CHRISTIE—THE ELOQUENT MAN

Tom Christie possessed a virtue I would consider classic eloquence, the God-given characteristic found in a combination of being comfortable in any situation, formal or informal, rich, non-affluent, specially talented or unskilled.

He had the forte of being the same Tom in all whereabouts, any longitude or latitude. He was the same everywhere—at home or any provincial territory. There are

Living with Loss

photos in his residence where his locale represents his leisure manners as well as in the tuxedo at his daughter's debutante party. I doubt if the human characteristics about which I write ever crossed his mind. They were built in, God created, and propelled.

A certain classic eloquence can be seen in the qualities of the loftiest office holders in the United States. Wherein such human being gifts and talents abound, one can observe such persons combining their ambitions with both the elite and down-to-earth instincts and surroundings. This goes on in some of our famous people's lives.

Consider two illustrations. Out of all the presidents of the United States, whereas their attributes were pretty much the same, one president, Dwight Eisenhower, while in the oval office of the United States, had the most outstanding position of all elegance, rank, and status on earth. Yet the element of unadornment shows up. Abilene, Kansas, at that time was a small town and community of some six thousand people. Dwight Eisenhower's love and passion for the spot where he was born and reared never faded. Abilene became the site of his presidential memorial and library, and in addition to this, his place of burial is just across the street from the footprints of his childhood and early life. There, the flavor of the casual easy-going community entombed his body with solemnity and ceremonial propriety. Visiting the site, for my wife and me, was moving. The Eisenhowers knew the suffering of losing a child, now included in the same memorial with his parents.

Another example unfolded in the life of former president Jimmy Carter. While he rubbed shoulders with leaders of other nations and was the center of attention like all persons holding the office he held, he never lost focus regarding his beginnings. He kept abreast of the small and simple village where his roots and appreciation penetrated his mind very deeply. Thus when his administration

James Thomas Christie Jr.

concluded in the highest office, a small town and community still guided his thinking. Likely out of all the classical and ornate stations he ever shared, the one most paramount was his small hometown, Plains, Georgia.

From Washington back to a small town of some 500 persons, he and Rosalyn returned. What did some classic country people come up with? Arrange some kind of masquerade with long tail coats and evening dresses? No! Such a celebration would indeed have been acceptable and proper. However, that did not happen.

Instead, the citizens of that area, or perhaps the Carters, birthed the idea of a covered dish supper. Perhaps it was the longest spread of food ever known anywhere. On the stage a country band played. All activity was a simple, classic engagement. Other Presidents and famous people have demonstrated simplicity and eloquence.

Tom Christie Jr. was reared in the city of Columbus, but his mother's childhood and background were embedded in a prominent family in a small community, Concord, Georgia. At that station was where he combined two natural instincts: time he spent developing and renovating log cabins along with his family, and sharing his plants, fruits and vegetables on the attractive property of his parents. Eloquence and classic simplicity, a desirable combination, manifested itself in his life, both a Godly gift in which he was thrilled and, at the same time, a blessing to others.

TOM CHRISTIE—THE BELIEVER

That evening of introduction, I met Tom the believer. The authentic belief he held was fashioned in the infancy period of his life. Tom's father was reared in a Southern Baptist

Living with Loss

Convention pastorium. Church life was a regular schedule in helping to shape the destiny of his faith. The fact he married into a parsonage family was something he looked upon as a territorial spark, rather than just trying to fit in. Thus he was a joy in his in-law's residence.

In the course of his rearing his own family, Sunday morning was a regular schedule of religious input in a large congregation. There was a section, front row area near the chancel, where he and his family were always positioned.

It was an exciting time for Tom Christie on three different occasions when his children were to be baptized as infants by his father-in-law in the Christian faith. He felt something monumental was transpiring in the interest of his children. His affirmation, religiously speaking, set up in the assurance of his creed. In humility he practiced a childlike faith—never bedecked or flourished—just the warmth of his heart.

Something happened in the life of Tom Christie which strongly cemented his reliance upon a power greater than he, a totally unexpected event—the catastrophe of the death of his only son. Any parent will in a flash tell you the kind of disaster Tom Jr. faced—the loss of a child, especially in the prime of life—is when the waters roar and a dream and a plan is eternally ended.

At this point a childlike faith in Tom's life began to take charge. Never did he show any consideration of straying from his course of faith in the Heavenly Father, to my knowledge. Never was there any detouring from the path of God or a weakening of his confidence in the Almighty. Actually it caused him to increase his stance at the post of his supposition about his salvation. Relationships to the doctrine and gospel which he held in esteem gave him strength in the bearing of such a burden.

Already opened is not only the account of yielding the son in whom he looked to his tomorrow regarding the

James Thomas Christie Jr.

extension of the family name, as we all do, but also at the time bearing the absence of his adorable companion through cancer.

However, one attribute he had left was his health plus two daughters. At least he could continue his loving profile. This was another serious reason for which to live. Again, no one suspected the responsibility and privilege passing to him would soon pass so quickly.

THE ILLNESS OF TOM CHRISTIE JR.

For long years, the Christie father had given his health serious attention. At the close of each day, he headed for the park two blocks away for physical therapy known as jogging.

His closeness to his youngest daughter caused the young daughter Ruth to accompany him on the track. It was at the period when a father in his late fifties realized his fifteen year old could surpass him in speed; this caused him to ponder, although her excellence was to be expected. Yet, when it did, the father noticed he was slipping, and thus all was not well. Someone mentioned to me, soon afterward, more bad news about the family!

At first, a devoted physician was hesitant to render any confirmed statement about the problem. Furthermore, the recent loss of Tom's beloved wife and son became almost now unbearable. Yes! For the third time in a span of a few years surrounding a reasonably youthful family, it was almost too much.

In referral recommendations and searching for a cause and effect of human treatment through drugs, Tom, like Joyce began going west (Texas). He was kindly supported with special aircraft travel and endless prayers.

The state our son-in-law encountered was that which so many of you have shared with your loved ones; mainly

LIVING WITH LOSS

lack of improvement in health. There are times when physical strength continues to weaken. Sometimes in our bodily conflict with health, when (healing) is not happening, our patience in returning to normalcy and feeling well again is short, and, to us, not acceptable. When day by day we cannot claim any progress and begin to realize a downward trend, the problem is worsened.

However, the original Tom the believer began to show up. Defeat in anything was never a part of his agenda. His upbeat expectancy of a better day never wavered. You can remember how someone in his or her suffering has been a role model for you when they themselves suffered for more than you or I. Tom dreamed of bouncing back, at the same time his good mind and wisdom, as in all of his previous misfortune, faced up in case what he preferred failed to materialize.

One day he said to me, "If I can just live two more years." I did not question him about placing hopeful time upon his life. Till this day, I believe I know why the yardstick of time came forth.

As a father, for one thing, he yearned to share his youngest child's life as a caring and supporting father until at least she finished high school. The hope to live only two years was, to me, such reasonable outlook, while it did not come to pass.

Yet he kept the faith—never complaining or questioning God. His strength lessened step-by-step as his health dethroned in a short time. Instead of jogging, there was the transition from running to a walking cane. This was followed by the assistance of a walker. Soon the walker was replaced for a wheelchair, etc.

One of the reasons I can write about this character in stability is he was so sturdy an adversary. The changing conditions were not measured by how he tip-toed through each move. Rather he walked forth. Anyone reading this report can speak of a loved one or a friend who, when in

James Thomas Christie Jr.

trouble, rather than causing depression, produced, instead, inspiration.

I listened recently to a person accidentally through radio who was employed in a government program known as Hospice. She is among those who spend their time caring for others. Said she, "My friends ask, 'do you not get depressed?'" Her answer, "No!" She continued, "I avoid being depressed through thinking that this is my calling." To help is to find satisfaction. Sharing a burden is rewarding.

Those of us who grow older expect to develop disorders in health. However, for those in the prime of life, surely it is more laborious.

Only a short time previously had this husband with his adorable wife bouldered through conversations they concluded (barring a miracle) soon they could not do together. These were decisions which needed to be made while leaning on each other. Neither of them in their best visionary perceived that in a matter of one-year span, the husband would (this time alone) be reviewing and facing further similar decisions about property, estate, future education of a fourteen-year-old; these and other determinations which had to be made now through singleness in mind. Yes, the treating of paperwork, establishing documentation in preparation, all of this the two went about with such nobility. They made it, in secular terms, to seem like business as usual. Maybe Joyce's goal for her life was that every day, "To God be the glory" gave them the strength which empowered the two through Jesus Christ to do almost the impossible.

Of course these were isolated periods of struggle, remorse, and tranquility. They must have again given thought to the words of George Matherson's hymn, "O Love That Will Not Let Me Go." This hymn was used in both of their funeral celebrations. "O Joy that seeketh me through pain, I cannot close my heart to thee; I trace the rainbow

Living with Loss

thru the rain, and feel the promise is not vain, that morn shall tearless be." (3rd stanza).

While the healing we all continued to hunger for was not coming through, something else very precious and beautiful was the multiple action of friends and relatives, young, middle-aged, seniors, everyone. While he grew worse, there was no way he could visit with all or receive the assistance so profoundly offered. In addition to his already suffering, he was disappointed in necessary withdrawal. He loved people. He had to give up, yet he never gave up.

On Wednesday afternoon, August 29, 1995, in his residence, I went to the threshold of his bedroom door. Aware of his tired body, I extended only an affectionate wave, as if to say "See you!"—inasmuch as he was seeing those to provide his physical care; our eyes met, Tom replied, "Come in, sit down, close the door."

My dear son-in-law could only manage slightly above a whisper; yet in fidelity and confidence, his commitment was "I'm not giving up."

He continued speaking in light of his primary concern, namely his daughters and our grandchildren, Brantley and Ruth. Said he, "Their welfare is covered." Then he remarked about their ownership of the family residence in which the five of them had played, loved, and received so many blessings.

The residence of which I have already alluded has always meant so much to me. All of us have preponderant places entwined in our hearts, bathed in eternal meaningfulness. Everyone has a castle somewhere. For thirty-two years, I had never visited them at any other address. They lived in longevity at 1546 Sixteenth Avenue. It was their place of abode, always. It was the wood structure of the early twenties where Tom had carried Joyce as his bride on June 16, 1963.

The conversation continued. Tom said, "You and I have both looked back too much. I can't do that anymore; I have

James Thomas Christie Jr.

only to look forward." At this point he released for me verbally some words I will never forget, but realize in some measure fulfills the Scripture. Said he, "There has to be a better place than this."

A little thought applied to his comment brings out the words of Jesus in St. John 14: 1-2. "Let not your heart be troubled; ye believe in God believe also in me. In my Father's house are many mansions. If it were not so, I would have told you, and if I go and prepare a place for you, I will come again and receive you unto myself; that where I am there you may be also." With perseverance he went on noting, "Both of us have looked back too much, today I must look forward."

This was followed by a devotional. Today I labor this pen in the same room of the Christie residence where this final prayer transpired. Sometimes there is a tear which quickly escapes through the power of precious memories. Not for a moment did I think that would be our final conversation. A conversation I almost missed. You can well recall some final verbal expression involving death which may not mean much for others, but for you is a genuine treasure.

Temporarily we returned to our residence. A call to his residence at noon on Saturday brought information from Jacob, a gentleman and employer, which reported his condition as stable. Three hours later, information revealed our dear Tom's heart had ceased to function.

As one reads this, there is one universal agreement about death. That is even when you know the hour is on the threshold, when the moment arrives and there are no more moments, that split second is more impounding than anticipated. The finality is more burdensome than what you had assumed. One is prepared and yet unprepared.

Lucile and I responded to the information as likely you have about a loved one. Our emotions stumbled. We were shaken by the closing of a book. We were so broken we were

LIVING WITH LOSS

little help to each other. The young man with simple, elegant, believing characteristics, a gentleman who had put together the loftiest of care for our daughter, (often I told them so) who could play, love, and support was no longer there in the flesh.

THE THIRD OF THREE WEEKENDS
SEPTEMBER 2-4, 1995

The third tragedy in a span of a few years had again occurred on a weekend in the Christie family. The same loving people, with their support, kept on being there for the third time in a fall atmosphere.

Tom had made it easy on his family all the way, at least in my presence, and I'm sure with others. In his great loss and his own mental anguish, he put his best foot forward. He simply remained far more cheerful and encouraging than one could expect.

To me, where he helped the most was in never showing any degree of rebellion. To be sure, no doubt, he had some questions, yet there was never any sign regarding hardening of the heart. The gentle attitude displayed in all of his life remained until his immortal transition.

On the Sunday following Tom's passing, people came and went all day from his home. The residence was where all contact with the family was made during each of the three tragic weekends.

On Sunday at the home, the pastor, Rev. Dr. Marion Edwards, who had officiated at the services on two Mondays in the past, raised the question about the ritual for Tom's service. Joyce, of course, had prepared for her own memorial service. He inquired if we had a copy.

For some reason, although not a thought in mind of the order of service being repeated, the Saturday before I had placed a copy in my automobile. When the pastor realized

James Thomas Christie Jr.

that a copy was available, he sat down with me for reviewing the material which Joyce had prepared. He chose to repeat the same content in the husband's service. He did so verbatim, except in the message itself.

For the third time the congregation and friends returned to the sanctuary just as they had done on Monday, October 10, 1988; Monday, October 4, 1993; and now on Monday, September 4, 1995.

The same great organ of musical splendor carried funeral entonements through the pipes, touched off by talented fingers. Each of us felt the loaded burden become a lighter burden as a multitude of mourners had gathered for the third time for the same family. They were shaken, somewhat devastated, but never yielded for a moment their support. The profound sadness, the frustration and bewilderment—nothing could dent their embracement in a time of need for a family hit so hard. Their response was enough in the time of such sorrow to make one cry for joy. The total number in the three gatherings was some twenty-four hundred.

Sixty miles from the Christie residence, north toward Atlanta, is a small, petite, well-manicured community called Concord. The filming of the movie, *Driving Miss Daisy,* was a main attraction in Concord in recent years. The Christie family has strong roots there.

In Concord and connected with the town begins a white four-panel fence. The wood enclosure on four sides and center section totals some three miles. Incumbered on the west end is a place of burial. The site is an uphill elevation. The long measure of fencing includes the town cemetery. Also in the barrier are lots upon which notable residential property has developed over the last few years. Many of the same pillar-like supports continued their adherence through making the trip to Concord.

At the peak of the hill, at the place of internment, one could think of Golgotha, not in the light of defeatism but rather like Jesus's final victory. Tom's tired and worn body was at last laid to rest beside his wife and son.

Today, from time to time, we are privileged to go there just as you do in the loss of loved ones. <u>As I have said before, the memories do not haunt us but help to make us.</u>

Also I bring to a close the memo I have penned about my son-in-law. I am working from a card table. It has dawned on me, as I inscribe these words sitting beside Tom's bed in the same room where our final conversation occurred, it certainly was not planned that this section of this book would finalize at this site. God does work in mysterious ways! Thus, I wish to claim the conclusion of these comments about Tom's life is the will of God and proposes honor to his name.

CHAPTER FOUR

Inheritance Through Illness and Death

EVER THOUGHT ABOUT ALL THE DIVERSE WAYS OUR LIVES ON the earth can and may terminate? Think of the circumstances of what caused us to lose a loved one or a friend. Or review the narrow escape that happened and could have caused my life or your life to be totally annihilated. I can readily recall incidents when my death could have taken place or my body deformed.

For instance, in youth, riding the horse species and being thrown over the animal's head upside down; leaping from trees into the river stream, not aware of water depth or other potential hazards; missed narrowly by an anchor chain dropped from a crane in a shipyard; accident on the highway and escaped by a narrow margin. Your report may read likewise, and yet we have had excess of life. Often a member of our generation has been severed from us through occurrences we never thought would happen.

While listening to a gentleman speaking long ago who was a medical doctor, perhaps I should have been embarrassed, never having given any thought to a truth the physician declared which was, is, and ever shall be, namely "everything living is dying." Of course, we all know so well from the day of our birth we begin the approachment to an earthly end.

None of us on the long pull know or can see down the road; the manner in which our lives on this planet will close. No doubt the most troublesome information we can receive is some medical prognosis predicting (due to some medical report) how long we are expected to live. However, one must quickly point out our scientific calculation may not be exactly what happens. Other controls take over, and the end results are better than anticipated.

There is no habitat of the flesh living today, no matter their wisdom, or their intelligence, who has improved (to my knowledge), with much satisfaction, our understanding of the mysteries and complexities of death and hereafter. That is not to say that the mental labors and searching by capable persons has proven invaluable, not at all. The legacy and insight of capable people have been rewarding and continues to prosper.

CONCERNING DEATH—WE CAN FACE IT

When we imply facing something painful and perplexing, we use the word *face*. The use of this figure of speech denotes treating, whatever is up front, foremost. The face, of course, is the most frontal aspect of the body.

Recently during the Christian Lenten season, in some sermon notes which I called "Jesus meeting the situation," I stated, "God is always preparing us for something we will have to face." Sometimes radiant joy and happiness. Sometimes melancholy on other labors reflecting evidence of hurt, loneliness, or despair. The Bible Scripture includes some four hundred references about the face. Jacob was finding help when he said, "For I have seen the Lord face to face" (Gen. 32:30). In humility Moses fell on

Inheritance Through Illness and Death

his face (Num. 16:4). At one point Jesus fell on his face and prayed. In each case a source of special power came aboard, providing new vitality.

Down the road a few miles on a farm was a prominent family representing all the good of life in its family values.

In that group of five, unexpectedly, the family was met with a jolting tragedy, sending four members into a daze and mental numbness. What happened was a teenage daughter, like many others, decided she no longer had any desire to live; the total imbalance of her mind took her life. Of course the mode of death multiplied the overwhelming suffering for the family. The parents were cast into another world. They joined the fraternity of worldwide adjustment for the first time: the loss of a child.

The same longing we all have to help each other drove me to the winsome residence. Soon after, the two siblings in the family, then college students, the father, and I were in a closed bedroom. A heartbroken dad of great character was cast in fragile emotions, struggling with the pain of death and the nature of loss.

Those of you who have experienced the death of a child in likewise circumstances arrive immediately into the same state of mind. The state of mind when remorse is compounded with self-inflicted censorship. Often a sense of guilt and self criticism becomes a double portion of grief.

That Saturday morning the other two daughters, also overshadowed with sorrow, suffering and trying to help with their dad, gave it their best. They were anxious to assure their father he was not to blame. "Don't say that Daddy." I want to think what I said was heaven sent, what a good man needed to hear. I was surprised by my own words in saying to my friend, whom I had known all my life, agreeing with him and calling my lifetime friend by name, I offered, "You are partially to blame." My words seemingly were well taken. The always very dependable

Living with Loss

father with newfound strength immediately stood up, pulled himself together with perfect posture, and said, "I must now face this."

No parent who has lost a child or grandchild through the child's own decision lives on without first feeling remorse and then censoring in their own lives. In the face of tragedy, anyone, regardless of level of innocence, becomes confessant. The remark I made, "Yes partly to blame," furthermore contained the following fact: Aren't we all and society as a whole indirectly to blame? Must be, because in the generation of my youth, such tragedy was unknown.

In the loss of a child, not only as mentioned above, but in other tragedies, we respond alike at the point of indictment directed at our own selves. While writing these pages, I pen these remarks in a very artistic residence. I'm upstairs in a very comfortable room. It was built like, perhaps, a room in your home, providing accommodations for a certain member of the family using what was once my grandson's place of abode, through high school, college, and afterwards. A photo of the young man, including all of his fraternity brothers, rests on the wall.

You have in your house, perhaps, the same or similar memories. I do pray your outlook in the loss of a loved one is like unto mine, not bathed altogether in melancholy through tears but also with a sense of honor and appreciation—where sorrow includes gratitude, where you can go on, where death can bring tears of peace, where memories are an asset to daily devotional. These reminders can be outlets of progress. In the grieving process, like any other state of mind, our good heavenly Father is present, not with any accusatory fixation, not ready to impeach us, but rather prompt and anxious to forgive us if in fact we did miss something. In his grace for us, there is not an impasse which cannot be managed, no uphill adversity which can consume us.

Inheritance Through Illness and Death

The Christies became a living example, proving to me and others how we can face death. Face to face they acknowledged terminal disease. Now, thirty years after signing their marriage license, they once again signed papers and documentation—paperwork which was such a joy earlier and now was so difficult. Taking care of what had to be done. Their attitude, although not business as usual, at times gave the impression of making things easier for their loved ones. I breathed a prayer of gratitude and wished my spiritual power was as strong as theirs. The two of them displayed the glory of God, working through plans for the future.

During my daughter's illness, her mother-in-law made the remark in my presence, "If God takes Joyce, I don't believe I can stand it." Another way of saying the same thing is, "I don't believe I can face it." Yet she did quite well.

During the Vietnam War, a wonderful mother in my congregation was enjoying life while sharing the blessing of two sons and a daughter. However, the beauty of fellowship with her family was interrupted through the horrible war. The U.S. military usually executes its responsibility about tragedy with tactful and passionate concern. In the following account, the procedure of report was made when one of the sons was lost in battle. The demeanor in which this mother was informed was contrary to normal governmental movement.

Through the night, the mother who lived alone following the death of her husband, heard a knock at the front door. In answering the messenger, a law enforcement officer held in his hand a manifest of horribly bad

Living with Loss

news. Her darling young son had been killed in action. Living alone, and being late at night, there was no one to share such communication. Mistakes are made, and the military should have sent a chaplain, which I'm sure they usually do. Also, perhaps they could have waited until morning. Not only was that horrifying and shocking bad news enough to break any mother, but, in addition, she had never before lost a child. Furthermore, there was the labor of waiting several weeks for her son's body. I claim we can face death as we observe other members of the family of God prove it can be done. The military, following that first fateful evening, gave their best in complete service.

The mother's younger son was also soldiering in the Vietnam conflict. During the memorial service in the church, as his brother's body was moved from the chancel, he stood in perfect form, squared his body, clothed in military uniform, and faced the casket while performing the military salutation. A perfect exercise, then facing the rest of his life never to know or share a daily relationship with a beloved brother.

At this very moment you have no difficulty in bringing to mind the response and actions of a friend in dealing with tragedy. Something on the surface would seem to be unmanageable and too hard to bear, yet he or she responded victoriously.

I do not find it boggling to the mind to understand how Joyce and Tom faced the impossible so gallantly. You see the answer is from time to time, when all was well (and certainly in misfortune), they knew what it was to be consoled through the presence of Jesus face to face. The example they left for their children, giving them strength and showing them how to confront hurt and pain, can glorify God.

It was only recently at the Christie residence I viewed the oldest daughter, dressed so couth while holding a flower

Inheritance Through Illness and Death

arrangement of beautiful roses. She appeared as a young woman with a mission. Her plan was to load a rental car, drive to Atlanta, and fly back to her work. Instead of taking the advantageous interstate, she chose a two-lane road. The road would lead to a cemetery on a hillside where she placed her flowers. Her mission was to be carried out alone, as she preferred.

Can you believe in her departure about the location and the site she was to approach, she said to me, "I love to go there."

By her statement, understandably, she did not imply her intentions included in any way a sense of joy. Her car loaded, she proceeded pleasantly. Our affections were expressed, and she drove away to fulfill her purpose alone. I thought, "How can you do it?" And yet I knew!

You see, in her unyielding faith, the Master did not let her go alone. In my selfishness, I wished in one sense I could have watched all of her movement. How gratifying that would have been. There was, however, the great one who pleasantly observed her affirmation, her goal in action as she faced her purpose so well. 'Tis nothing new to say: through Jesus we can face the most trying of all trials.

CONCERNING DEATH—WE CAN ACCEPT IT

One level of acceptance about any word, deed, or thing carries the meaning of approval. However, in responding to something so serious as death, acceptance does not always mean approval or necessarily imply sanction. Often there are burdensome conditions whence we would not feel comfortable through the comment, "I approve." On the other hand, in the same condition we can venture, "I accept what is unchangeable."

LIVING WITH LOSS

When something has happened to us, one might say, "It's just as well . . . accept it. There is no choice!" That interpretation is both true and false. Often there is some degree of choice. Almost without exception we have an option. Through our own volition we made a determination; we pick a course. For the most part, there is always a crossroad. A well known prayer reads:

> God grant me
> the serenity to accept the things I cannot change,
> the courage to change the things I can
> and the wisdom to distinguish
> between the two.

There are exceptional circumstances; for instance, prison sentences by law are not optional. In some circumstances we cannot be selective. Normal death when due to longevity of life is not territory where we can be selective. Although there are choices sometimes in sustaining life through mechanical devices.

The following illustration is not the area of foreign relations. The scene I'm about to reveal is not distant territory; most people have been there.

The date was September 16, 1993, in the year of our Lord A.D. In the late afternoon there was a gathering of four persons. The setting was totally offhand and unexpected. Our very ill daughter shifted locations as she moved from the library to a sitting location in her residence and sat down in a soft chair. Her father, mother, and sister were all in the area, and the four of us came together. Three of us were on our knees surrounding the chair where Joyce sat. Our presence merged

Inheritance Through Illness and Death

into one there as we all faced each other. What occurred was perhaps like some experience you have shared. We heard a wonderful mother's voice, clear and distinct. Her remarks were in regards to her youngest child, "first it was the death of her brother, now it is her mother. I do not understand."

Sometimes if someone is in serious trouble, dealing not only with finality of earthly existence but other mental agitations, then the mind goes into mutiny, unhealthy, revolting. Yet our daughter, like Jesus, accepted the burden. Others have done likewise. When this happens, acceptance becomes very disquieting. Such is only a part of mind and soul reflected in the meaningfulness of believers. Our daughter's acceptance glorified God and made for her family a lighter burden.

DEATH—WE CAN ADJUST TO IT

During the closing chapter of Tom Christie Jr.'s life on earth, new neighbors arrived on Sixteenth Avenue. Most any person purchasing or buying residential property near Tom Christie did not need to go seeking his acquaintance. Tom, in his hospitable manner and desire to help, crossed the street first, at times before transition of property occurred. The warmth of his personality helped others to settle in. Fresh neighbors responded accordingly. Mr. Christie, although in his fifties, held seniority in that vicinity. There Tom was the greeter who welcomed others to the neighborhood. Such was the case when two doors down, Barbara Johnson, a single parent, and Ryan, her ten-year-old son, came aboard.

Barbara and Ryan arrived from Oregon. The lad was enrolled in the structure and framework of Christian Catholicism. Following Mr. Christie's death, Barbara sent me a paper written by her twelve-year-old son. The heartfelt illustration was a model of coping with anger caused by

LIVING WITH LOSS

> *Thursday 9/4/95*
>
> Sometimes the Lord calms the storm; sometimes He lets the storm rage and calms His child.
>
> This reminds me of when my neighbor Tom Gustie died. He had this disease called Lou Gehrig's Disease. I had been praying for him to get better. Then one day he stopped breathing. I was very angry, but later I calmed down because I knew Tom was in heaven.

> *Monday 10/2/95*
>
> God always gives His best to those who leave the choice with Him.
>
> Psalm 68:19
>
> God will always favor those who trust him. When our next door neighbor became sick, I prayed that he would recover. One day he died. I was mad at God, but I realized he was finally cured. He was in a place where there is eternal happiness, heaven.
>
> I still cry for him because I miss him. But I trust in God and know that his decision for him to die was the best for him.

Above is a copy of what twelve-year-old Ryan Johnson wrote for two assignments.

Inheritance Through Illness and Death

unavoidable circumstances. The paper was the result of an assignment prepared in his own words in response to a certain passage of Scripture. The following are copies of what Ryan had written. They are repetitive. However, I prefer to use both. I have his permission.

Thursday 9/14/95

Sometimes the Lord calms the storm; sometimes He lets the storm rage and calms His child.

This reminds me of when my neighbor Tom Cristie died. He had this disease called Lou Gerig's Disease. I had been praying for him to get better. Then one day he stopped breathing. I was very angry, but later I calmed down because I knew Tom was in heaven.

Monday 10/2/95

God always gives His best to those who leave the choice with Him.

Psalm 68:19

God will always favor those who trust him. When our next door neighbor became sick, I prayed that he would recover. One day he died. I was mad at God, but I realized he was finally cured. He was in a place where there is eternal happiness, heaven.

I still cry for him because I miss him. But I trust in God and know that his decision for Tom to die was the best for him.

In the book of Isaiah the eleventh chapter, sixteenth verse, God makes reference to Jesus as a child when he states, "A little child shall lead them." All over the land there are thoughts of young children producing movements and creating something helpful for us all. Ryan

LIVING WITH LOSS

was reporting how he faced a neighbor's death and adjusted to it.

ADJUSTING TO DEATH THROUGH INHERITANCE

By inheritance, not by any consideration do I think of earthly inheritance. Some may receive through legacy or perishable estate, which is desirable and often God sent. Yet physical birthright is not the heritage the above Scripture supposes. The kind of heir relationship God offers is not that of hand-me-downs but rather hand-me-ups. Coexistence with God is inheritance where there is no termination, no misunderstanding, or no dissatisfaction—inheritance where God's will is always just and glorious, and family members are at peace together.

We inherit memories we would not exchange for gold and silver. They are more precious than rubies and diamonds. Your parents and my parents taught us values from which we gain strength.

Earlier in this publication I mentioned a time I had alone with Joyce. Prayer was instilled in her life. Said she, "Daddy I want you to pray the prayer of salvation and pray that I won't suffer." We did! So our prayer was answered.

You and I have known persons with great spiritual depth. Joyce reached the most eminent relationship with our Savior than any person I've ever known, including her father. Yes, our loved ones often leave us a life to be copied, a book to be read, a blessing in living with loss.

> The spirit itself beareth witness with our spirit that we are children of God. And if children, then heirs; heirs of God, and joint heirs with Christ; if so be that we suffer with him that we may also be glorified together, for I reckon that the sufferings of the present times are not worthy to be compared to the glory which shall be revealed in us. (Rom. 8:16–18)

Inheritance Through Illness and Death

I walked down the street in the late 1950s where unexpected death had come to pass involving one of the upfront families in a charming county seat town. The home to which I was going was that of some Baptist friends—husband and wife who were the proprietors of a downtown business and, up until a few hours previously, had never lost a child. A young man earlier had become a part of the family when united through marriage. A beautiful relationship had arisen resulting in the son-in-law becoming a partner in the family enterprise.

A few days earlier his young wife had been hospitalized. Her problem seemingly was routine recovery. Something went wrong, and her death brought melancholy to the entire community. I went to the home. Upon entering the red brick residence, what I anticipated never materialized.

From the front door, I was shown to the mother's bedroom. I wasn't prepared for the omen. A mother so torn and upset was what one would expect. Instead I viewed a mother's radiant and smiling face. She said to me, "Preacher, all my life I've heard the comment through a daughter's words, 'I want to follow in my mother's footsteps.' Today you are looking at a mother who wants to follow in her daughter's footsteps." It was as if the mother was saying, through my daughter a chapter has been handed down to me, whose life I expect to copy.

Terminologywise the usual had become the unusual. Her language lodged in the center of my brain, while her smiling face rested in the center of my heart. Verbally her words were so positive. I could until this day return to the grounds where a mother sat in a chair, her back to the north side of the house, and freely committed herself to write in her book of life a rerun of her daughter's life, even though brokenhearted in her loss.

There is always some pursuit of movement in the heritage process. Secularly speaking, the transition of property becomes active at the time of death. Likewise the

LIVING WITH LOSS

spiritual proposition comes into play. How often have you heard the words while coping with tragedy: "I just try to keep busy." Any individual has a better opportunity while adjusting to loss through death if blessed with mobile movement. The same is true of spiritual response. This mother recognized her spiritual inheritance. In this regard, there are opportunities, we can execute and find consolation; performances we can, through memories, make happen and find gratification. Jesus unto his disciples in St. Luke 22:19 stated, "This do in remembrance of me." How frequently we notice followers of our Lord find strength through making response to this request centuries later. It brings validity to the soul.

As for me, I feel fortunate I can return to burial sites of family members with a reasonable outlook, though well do I know that in this privileged movement not everyone can manage. These are movements not everyone can attain.

On the premises where we have lain our loved ones' bodies to rest, as some family members return to the site, it helps to meet their need, but for others the thought is negative. However, I assure you, it can without forewarning change for the better, and a presence where the body is preserved can settle in the heart and, therefore, bring peace of mind.

Of course some may feel (and rightly so) the gravesite represents our cessation of life on earth; thus, spirit is not there and visits are not essential. Let us remember, we place overwhelming emphasis on flesh while on earth, as it should be. Therefore, why not remember the earthly body? Such exercise can integrate emphasis on soul and body, bringing desirable thoughts into balance as they come together. A sense of peace intercedes although the cemetery is only a door to the immortal; yet it is a station that becomes a refuge and something of a sanctuary where needs may be met.

Inheritance Through Illness and Death

If you and I were in an assembly where open testimony of graveside experiences were being shared, we would be inspired through accountable reports; occurrences (some might consider illusions) yet accounts which magnify the reality of life beyond the grave. Please bear witness to the following two accounts.

My wife and I parked our automobile on one occasion and strolled together for support to two graves (at that time) and later the third. The mother of Joyce Christie rested on the molding of an elevated stone marker. I stood by the graves. Something happened! Something good!

My wife and I always engage in worship orally during such visits. I was reading aloud from Joyce's selection from her memorial service, "How Great Thou Art" second stanza, "When through the woods and forest glades I wonder and hear the birds sing sweetly in the trees." My wife interrupted and said, "Ernest, listen to that!"

A cluster of birds had flown into the cemetery lighting near the grave with feet on the ground, fluttering, singing, and chirping. Then, as quickly as they had appeared, they took flight and vanished.

What shaped this mysterious circumstance even more is there is little vegetation on that particular earthly site. The birds positioned themselves on bare soil where there was no growth. The two of us were spiritually moved through what had transcended. The tears on our cheeks turned into lofty and holy smiles, as we walked away hand-in-hand. God had directed angelic song birds, a feathered tribal unit, to bring solace and peace in a special form, something he does for all his children.

The second manifestation (later) of two unique experiences in spiritual domain was as follows. It was the day when a spiritual body was detached from an earthly body and became, briefly, a heavenly manifestation. A body in spiritual form. As my wife and I stood beside the memorial site, immediately before my face our daughter arose

LIVING WITH LOSS

from the grave with a shining countenance, whence she confirmed a truth very emphatically! The flesh had become spirit.

Joyce stood immediately in front of me. Then with her arm at chest level, she extended her medium-size hand and with the forefinger pointed directly at the physical location of my heart and pleasantly stated, "I'm not here. I'm right there in your heart." Just as quickly her body retreated to her previous position, the grave.

One can imagine how my mood was altered. I received a spiritual adjustment. Everything became radiant. A daughter through death proving God is real. My need that day was met. A proclamation of life beyond the grave.

Yes, by an individual who seemingly had no power, yet through the grace of God became all powerful. In St. John 20:19, 26, Jesus returned in body and stood in the midst of his disciples for the sole purpose of reassuring them, cementing their faith. Also on one occasion, while Mary was weeping at the tomb, she experienced her faith convincingly certified when Jesus suddenly appeared in spiritual form.

I'm of the thinking that in the spiritual extension of your loved ones, something has occurred strengthening your confidence although totally unanticipated. Yes, a cemetery can be the crossroads where God is waiting without planned procedure.

Without a doubt our paths are waiting in the hills of Golgotha, though problematic. Our paths often bisect the path of God while he waits to assure us of his presence. After all, Jesus gave time for a place we adore, a vineyard we maintain, yes even a cemetery. Mary wept by the side of the grave, hurt and disappointed. She had no idea she would hear the most reassuring words she had ever heard; the words of Jesus as he called her by name. There was an exchange of relationship between her and her Lord blessing her soul.

Inheritance Through Illness and Death

Another active resource we can put in motion is directed monetary process. Often God's servants have an opportunity to contribute funds toward establishing some immortal memorial which perpetrates a name into extension.

In 1941, my wife and I made a wise decision to tithe our income, as others have done, ten percent of our earnings. The decision put us in a state to make a sizeable contribution in her memory, agreeable with her prior to her eternal transition. Perhaps you have done likewise.

Often survivors can do something for each other.

Following three tragedies, at one point we were in the family residence spending some time in the library. Whereupon the youngest daughter Ruth entered the area. In her hands she carried a Bible.

She appeared to be a teenager with a purpose. Reaching our presence, she announced her plans. "Here Grandmother, I have something for you." Her grandmother reached out her hands as she received a very precious heritage. The teen presented the Holy Book as a gift to her grandmother. Her own mother's Holy Bible, which will probably be returned into the youth's hand someday—the grandmother back to the granddaughter.

In looking through pages of Joyce's Holy Bible, Lucile came upon treasured material including such as follows:

"God is enough."

She also found other writings, including a handwritten prayer. I do not know whether they were personal writings or not, but they reflect Joyce's devotion and faith. It is a comfort to have these words as a remembrance.

Teach me the glory of my Cross;
Teach me the Value of my thorn,
Show me that I have Climbed
to thee by the path of my pain.
Show me that my tears have
made my rainbows.

April 8, 1987

(Found in Joyce's Bible)

Inheritance Through Illness and Death

It is always amazing how death brings us together, as has already been stated. We can become a support group. Often one person will establish a relationship with another. You will never know what a blessing you have been to people like me. The person being addressed has received from the person seeking equal help.

Your reply to death has often moved you to do something assuring for a person or persons of your desired accountability. You set in motion a prayer, a deed, or a word—you become energetic in passion. "What can I do?" We can offer.

Thus for each other there is an involuntary chain of embracements, creating consolation and encouragement, as we hurt together. Often little deeds, brief comments, and memorials contribute to our needs.

Perhaps an unexcelled idea set in motion by someone and propelled into action by many in regard to the Christie family brought family survivors to their knees in humble gratitude.

The motion included new development of landscaping for the church grounds of St. Luke United Methodist Church.

The new landscaping was to be called, "The Christie Gardens." The project necessitated a large sum of money.

What created an attitude of meekness for the Christie's loved ones was additionally energized by the unselfish generosity and spirit of the long established St. Luke congregation and friends.

What is meant by the proceeding statement can be best interpreted through the following. Usually a project through an earmarked stone and inscription lifts up a name of person or family from generation to generation of longevity in a congregation. In this case the Veal–Christie name was fairly young in the St. Luke Church and the only family of those names.

I suppose one can say the project adopted by the church administration is somewhat justified through the

LIVING WITH LOSS

The Christie Gardens

Dedicated to the Glory of God and in Loving Memory O

James Thomas Christie, III
Joyce Veal Christie
James Thomas Christie

"I Thank My God on All Remembrance of You."
(Philippians 1:3)

Inscription on the stone for the garden.

magnitude of tragedy in the Christie family. Nevertheless it was, is, and always shall be a generous gesture, leaving the family to feel—tongues cannot tell or lips cannot recite the gratitude felt for a noble act through which a heavy burden has been altered, made lighter indeed. A kind thought through action certainly.

In bringing to a close this section of this book and final words on inheritance, I am fully aware that in the loss of a child there are parents in every community who miss a son or daughter who was their only child. Under those conditions the vacant spot is accelerated in grief. We are more fortunate. We have another desirable daughter and son plus another inspiring grandson and pleasant son-in-law.

We also have beautiful inheritance through the gift of Brantley and Ruth. They have managed their seemingly

Inheritance Through Illness and Death

unsurmountable tragedies admirably. Just as your grandchildren are an inspiration to you, ours are to us. The four of us cling together. Financially, their parents provided for their needs down the road. One of the treasures in our hands is a copy of the spiritual brilliance of our daughter's soul, while she was ill, in preparation of celebration in her death and used in the memorial service.

Since 1993 her parents use sections of her eulogy material each morning at breakfast hour as devotional for the day. An exercise we plan to use so long as we shall live.

Yes, in illness and death as you well know, we can live with loss.

WORDS OF COMFORT

It is my hope that you will find comfort in these passages which were Joyce's favorites and which I feel are befitting to her coexistence with God:

> I have fought a good fight,
> I have finished my course,
> I have kept the faith.
> Henceforth there is laid up for me
> a crown of righteousness. (2 Tim. 4:7–8)

> When I was a child, I spoke as a child,
> I understood as a child, I thought as a child,
> but when I became a man I put away childish things.
> For now I see through a glass, darkly,
> but then face to face. (1 Corin. 13:11–12)

LIVING WITH LOSS

The Lord God is my strength
and he will make my feet like hinds' feet,
and he will make me
to walk upon high places. (Hab. 3:19)

For I reckon that the sufferings
of the present time shall not be compared
to the glory which shall be
revealed in us. (Rom. 8:18)

Let not your heart be troubled:
Ye believe in God,
believe also in me. (John 14:1)